A LETTER OF
RESIGNATION

For Rohan
with my love

HUGH WHITEMORE

A LETTER OF
RESIGNATION

AMBER LANE PRESS

All rights whatsoever in this play are strictly reserved and application for
professional performance should be made before rehearsals begin to:
Judy Daish Associates Ltd,
2 St Charles Place,
London W10 6EG

Application for amateur performance should be made before rehearsals begin to:
Samuel French Ltd,
52 Fitzroy Street,
London W1P 6JR

No performance may be given unless a licence has been obtained.

First published in 1997 by
Amber Lane Press Ltd,
Church Street, Charlbury, Oxford OX7 3PR
Telephone: 01608 810024

Printed and bound by
The Guernsey Press Co Ltd, Guernsey, C.I.

ISBN 1 872868 22 3

CHARACTERS

(in order of appearance)

MRS BRENNAN

OLIVER WIDDOWES

IAN RITCHIE

LADY DOROTHY MACMILLAN

HAROLD MACMILLAN

The play is set in the library of a castle in Scotland
during an evening in the summer of 1963.

A Letter of Resignation is a work of fiction. Harold Macmillan
was told of Mr Profumo's resignation by telephone and not by
emissaries from London. Widdowes, Ritchie and Mrs Brennan
are invented characters. Nevertheless the main events
described and discussed actually happened and are fully
documented.

A Letter of Resignation was first presented by Duncan C. Weldon at the Yvonne Arnaud Theatre, Guildford, on 9th September 1997, and subsequently by Duncan C. Weldon with Alexander H. Cohen and Max Cooper at the Comedy Theatre, London, on 16th October 1997, with the following cast:

HAROLD MACMILLAN ... Edward Fox
LADY DOROTHY MACMILLAN ... Clare Higgins
OLIVER WIDDOWES ... Julian Wadham
IAN RITCHIE ... John Warnaby
MRS BRENNAN ... Doreen Andrew

Director: Christopher Morahan
Designer: Eileen Diss
Lighting: Mick Hughes
Costumes: Tom Rand
Sound: Tom Lishman

The curtain rises to reveal the library of a castle in Scotland. A comfortable room with untidily crowded bookshelves, squashy-cushioned chairs and oldish paintings on the walls. Drinks and glasses stand on a table beside the telephone.

It is an evening in the summer of 1963.

The door opens and the housekeeper, MRS BRENNAN, comes in with a middle-aged Englishman, OLIVER WIDDOWES. He is wearing a well-cut but slightly crumpled suit and carrying a briefcase. MRS BRENNAN, whose neat grey hair has been permed recently, is wearing a discreet party dress.

MRS BRENNAN   Would you like to wait in here, sir, or would you rather go to your room?

WIDDOWES   I'll wait here. Thank you.

MRS BRENNAN   Sir Patrick asked me to apologise for not coming to meet you himself. There's a special dinner being held in the barn.

WIDDOWES   Yes, he explained when I telephoned.

MRS BRENNAN   Mr McFee's retiring. As soon as Sir Patrick knew the Prime Minister was coming to stay, he decided to have a special retirement party. The Prime Minister and Mr McFee have often been shooting together.

WIDDOWES   Yes, yes, I know.

MRS BRENNAN   There's going to be a presentation after dinner and then dancing. It's quite an occasion. Sir Patrick hopes you'll be able to join him later, sir, after your meeting with the Prime Minister.

WIDDOWES   I'm not sure if that'll be possible, but I'll certainly
do so if I can. Do thank Sir Patrick, won't you,
and please give my best wishes to Mr McFee.

MRS BRENNAN Yes, sir, of course. Would you like something to
eat, sir?

WIDDOWES   Not at the moment, thank you. Go back to the
party, Mrs Brennan. You're missing all the fun.

MRS BRENNAN Thank you, sir.

[*She goes to the door.*]

In case you're wondering, sir —the other gentleman's having a lie down.

WIDDOWES   What other gentleman?

MRS BRENNAN Mr Ritchie.

WIDDOWES   Who's Mr Ritchie?

MRS BRENNAN I thought he was a colleague of yours, sir. He said
he missed the train from London. That's why he
came up on a plane.

WIDDOWES   I don't know a Mr Ritchie.

MRS BRENNAN He didn't look at all well. I think the plane upset
his stomach. I gave him cup of tea and told him
to have a lie down.

WIDDOWES   Quite right.

MRS BRENNAN You're sure there's nothing you want, sir?

WIDDOWES   I'd like to ring my wife — is that possible?

MRS BRENNAN The telephone's over there, sir, on the table.

WIDDOWES   Ah, yes. Thank you, Mrs Brennan.

MRS BRENNAN Thank you, sir.

[MRS BRENNAN *exits.*]

[WIDDOWES *goes to the telephone and dials for
the operator.*]

WIDDOWES Hullo? —Yes, could I have a London number, please? Bayswater 5253 — Thank you.

> [*There is a pause while* WIDDOWES *waits for the call to be connected. He stares at his reflection in a wall mirror and straightens his tie. The call is answered.*]

Darling, it's me — Yes, I'm here. At long last. The journey was hellish. I had to change at Glasgow — No, no, I haven't seen him yet. There's a dinner for old McFee, remember him? He's retiring and they're giving him a party.

> [*Unseen by* WIDDOWES, *the door opens and* IAN RITCHIE *enters. He is about 35. He is wearing a suit which is, perhaps, just a little too fashionable to pass muster in White's or Brooks's. He is carrying a briefcase.*]

Did the office ring? — I'm bit puzzled. A man called Ritchie has turned up. Apparently from London. God knows who he is. Might be a new boy in the Press Office, I suppose, though I can't imagine what he's doing here — What? — Well, I'm assuming I'll see the PM after dinner. I'm rather dreading it — Thank you, darling — Is everything all right? No problems? — Good — Yes, yes, I'll ring in the morning. Take care of yourself. Much love. Goodnight.

> [*He hangs up. He turns and sees* RITCHIE *smiling at him.*]

RITCHIE Hullo. I'm Ritchie. Ian Ritchie. You must be Oliver Widdowes.

WIDDOWES Yes. How do you do.

> [*They shake hands.*]

RITCHIE   All a bit of a cock-up, I'm afraid. They sent me off to Euston and I missed the bloody train. I had to fly up. Dreadful. One of those little private planes. Like a mini with wings. God, I felt sick. I never want to see Carlisle from the air again. I thought my last hour had come.

WIDDOWES   How are you feeling now?

RITCHIE   Much better, thanks. Mrs Danvers fussed around and got me a cup of tea. I was rather hoping for a Scotch.

           [*He grins and goes to the window.*]

           There's some sort of a do going on in the barn. A knees-up for one of the family retainers. Incredibly feudal. Amazing, isn't it, that sort of life still going on.

WIDDOWES   Do forgive me. I don't know who you are.

RITCHIE   Ritchie. MI5.

WIDDOWES   MI5...?

RITCHIE   Didn't they tell you I was coming?

           [WIDDOWES *is annoyed.*]

WIDDOWES   They did not.

           [RITCHIE *responds with a casual shrug.*]

RITCHIE   You know how it is. Things crop up. The Prime Minister might have some questions.

WIDDOWES   All that stuff can be dealt with in London.

RITCHIE   The Director-General thought otherwise.

WIDDOWES   This is ridiculous. Did he speak to Mr Butler about it?

RITCHIE   I suppose he must've done.

WIDDOWES   The Prime Minister is going to find your presence very disturbing.

RITCHIE   It wasn't my idea —

WIDDOWES   You know how he dislikes the Security Service. It would've been far better to let me handle this alone.

RITCHIE   It wasn't my idea to come rushing up to Scotland. Totally buggered up my day. Tomorrow, too, I suppose, travelling back. How long's it take by train?

WIDDOWES   Ten hours.

RITCHIE   Bloody hell.

WIDDOWES   If you're lucky.

RITCHIE   God.

[*Pause.*]

WIDDOWES   Her name is Mrs Brennan, by the way, not Mrs Danvers. The housekeeper.

RITCHIE   It was supposed to be a joke. Mrs Danvers is the housekeeper in *Rebecca*. The Daphne du Maurier story. Mrs Danvers is the creepy housekeeper.

[*No response from* WIDDOWES. *Pause.* RITCHIE *looks at the drinks.*]

Do you think it'd be all right if we helped ourselves?

WIDDOWES   I'm sure Paddy wouldn't mind.

RITCHIE   Want one?

WIDDOWES   Please. Gin and tonic.

[RITCHIE *pours drinks.*]

RITCHIE   Do you work directly for the Prime Minister?

WIDDOWES   I do.

RITCHIE   As one of his Private Secretaries?

WIDDOWES   Correct.

RITCHIE   What does that mean exactly?

            [*He gives a gin and tonic to* WIDDOWES *and pours a Scotch for himself.*]

WIDDOWES   Thank you. What does it mean...?

RITCHIE   I can't believe you do shorthand and typing.

            [WIDDOWES *responds with a chilly smile.*]

WIDDOWES   Not exactly.

RITCHIE   Is it a political appointment or are you a Civil Servant?

WIDDOWES   The Private Secretaries are part of the Prime Minister's personal staff. We try to make sure that his office is run smoothly and efficiently. We offer guidance and advice. It's all too easy for a Prime Minister to become isolated from the real world. It's our job to keep him in touch.

RITCHIE   How do you do that?

WIDDOWES   By telling him the truth.

RITCHIE   And do you?

WIDDOWES   On the whole.

            [*The two men sip their drinks.*]

RITCHIE   What do you make of the girl?

WIDDOWES   What girl?

RITCHIE   Miss Keeler. Rather a tasty piece, don't you think? Very sultry. The sultry Miss Keeler. Talk about hypocrisy. Everyone saying tut-tut, how appalling, whereas, in fact, they're all dying to get her into bed. All the chaps, anyway. We had the FBI sniffing around last week. They seem to think she might've had a fling with President Kennedy. Lucky sod.

WIDDOWES I don't think we should talk about this until we've discussed it with the Prime Minister.

RITCHIE Fair enough. [*He sips his Scotch.*] I gather he's a friend of yours.

WIDDOWES Who?

RITCHIE Our host. Sir Patrick.

WIDDOWES Why do you gather that?

RITCHIE You called him Paddy.

WIDDOWES We were at school together.

RITCHIE Well of course. [*He smiles, amused.*] I wonder at what level it is that going to the same school becomes a social advantage?

WIDDOWES At what level...?

RITCHIE Being at Eton or Winchester clearly means a great deal. Nobody gives a damn if you went to Hastings Grammar.

WIDDOWES No doubt you disapprove.

RITCHIE Not in the least. The English class system exists because we find it indispensable. Wouldn't you say? It satisfies some profound sociological need. Probably because we're all so lazy.

WIDDOWES What's that got to do with it?

RITCHIE It means we can blame our failures and misfortunes on an accident of birth without feeling obliged to do anything about it.

[*The door opens and* LADY DOROTHY *comes in, followed by her husband, the Prime Minister,* HAROLD MACMILLAN. *They are wearing evening dress.*]

[MACMILLAN *is in his late sixties;* LADY DOROTHY *is a few years younger.*]

[*Imitations of the Macmillans should be avoided. They should have their own existence as characters and not as mere impersonations. Nevertheless, it is important to remember* MACMILLAN'*s studied Edwardian languor and* LADY DOROTHY'*s deliberate avoidance of anything that might be regarded as elegant or fashionable.*]

LADY DOROTHY   Oliver, dear, how nice to see you. I won't ask why you're here. I'm sure it's enormously confidential.

WIDDOWES   Hullo, Lady Dorothy. Hullo, sir.

MACMILLAN   Good evening, Oliver.

WIDDOWES   This is Mr Ritchie. Lady Dorothy Macmillan. The Prime Minister.

LADY DOROTHY   How do you do.

RITCHIE   How do you do.

MACMILLAN   Sorry, I didn't catch your name.

RITCHIE   Ritchie, sir.

LADY DOROTHY   Sir Patrick said you weren't very well. Are you feeling better?

RITCHIE   Yes, thank you.

LADY DOROTHY   It's a beastly thing, travel sickness.

MACMILLAN   One of our grandchildren is always sick in motor cars.

LADY DOROTHY   We give him barley sugar; it seems to work. Ask Mrs Brennan for some barley sugar.

MACMILLAN   I'm told Ruskin recommended jumping as a cure for sea-sickness.

LADY DOROTHY   We're not talking about sea-sickness, Harold. Mr Ritchie came in a plane.

MACMILLAN   The principle might be the same.

LADY DOROTHY   How could it be? One can't jump up and down in an aeroplane. [*to* RITCHIE] Take my advice: stick to barley sugar. [*to* WIDDOWES] Have you heard about the party they're giving for McFee?

WIDDOWES   Yes, I gather he's retiring.

LADY DOROTHY   Seventy next month. Looks forty.

MACMILLAN   [*to* RITCHIE] The best grouse keeper I've ever known. A fifteen thousand acre beat and all he's got is a bicycle. Last year there were fifty-three days of top-quality shooting. You can't ask for better than that. Are you a shooting man?

RITCHIE   I'm afraid not.

[LADY DOROTHY *laughs.*]

LADY DOROTHY   That reminds me of Selwyn's wonderful story.

MACMILLAN   What does?

LADY DOROTHY   Asking Mr Ritchie if he's a shooting man.

MACMILLAN   What are you talking about?

LADY DOROTHY   You remember.

MACMILLAN   A story about Selwyn?

LADY DOROTHY   Not about him. A story he told us. About the Russians. [*to* RITCHIE] When Selwyn Lloyd was Foreign Secretary, he gave a luncheon for Bulganin and Khruschev.

MACMILLAN   Oh *that* story.

LADY DOROTHY   You remember?

MACMILLAN   Yes, yes, of course.

LADY DOROTHY   They were having lunch, you see, or were about to have lunch, having drinks and so forth, and Selwyn introduced Khruschev to his PPS, Tony Lambton. "This is Lord Lambton," he said, "our 'shooting' Lord."

MACMILLAN   Tony's a damn good shot. Outstanding.

LADY DOROTHY   The Russian translator translated into Russian, and suddenly Khruschev began to behave very strangely. He became tremendously solemn and kept looking at Tony with a tremendously mournful expression. Selwyn couldn't think what was wrong — until somebody told him that the Russian translator wasn't much good at his job, and when he tried to translate 'shooting Lord' he had, in fact, told Khruschev that Tony was about to be shot!

               [*Everyone laughs.*]

MACMILLAN   I wonder if Khruschev understood the joke. He has a very unpredictable sense of humour.

LADY DOROTHY   I'm sure he's unpredictable in every way. And so ugly. I know that shouldn't matter, but it does.

MACMILLAN   I always think of him as a cross between Peter the Great and Lord Beaverbrook.

LADY DOROTHY   I wouldn't trust him an inch.

MACMILLAN   That goes without saying. [*to* RITCHIE] When I visited the Soviet Union in 1959, I discovered the Russian for 'good day' sounds very like 'double gin'. Dobri dyen — double gin. So I went round

Russia, wearing a fur hat, smiling at everyone and saying 'double gin, double gin'. It was a great success.

[*Laughter.* LADY DOROTHY *goes to the door.*]

LADY DOROTHY I must let you get on with your meeting. [*to* RITCHIE] Have you had a chance to look at the gardens? — They're quite marvellous.

RITCHIE Not yet, no.

LADY DOROTHY The most marvellous rhododendrons. Do have a look. The soil's perfect here, of course, and there's enough shelter to protect them from the frost. They had a dreadful frost this year, Paddy says, the worst he's ever known — but the rhododendrons survived. Quite remarkable. Do have a look in the morning. [*to* MACMILLAN] You won't be too long, will you?

MACMILLAN No, no. [*to* WIDDOWES] I've got to say a few words and give McFee his clock or whatever it is.

LADY DOROTHY A teapot. Queen Anne. Very handsome. [*to* WIDDOWES] How's Isobel?

WIDDOWES Much better, thank you; we're all very hopeful.

LADY DOROTHY Oh good. Do give her my love. [*to* RITCHIE] I'm sure we'll meet again before you go back to London.

RITCHIE I hope so, Lady Dorothy.

[LADY DOROTHY *exits.*]

[*A moment of silence.*]

MACMILLAN I thought Rab Butler was supposed to be taking care of everything. What disaster has sent you scurrying up to Perthshire?

WIDDOWES   Mr Profumo came to see us. It seems he did sleep with that girl after all. He lied to Parliament.

[MACMILLAN, *although shocked, makes no response.* WIDDOWES *takes a letter from his brief-case.*]

This is his letter of resignation.

[*He gives the letter to* MACMILLAN, *who opens the envelope, takes out the letter and reads it carefully. He walks to the window and looks out at the darkening landscape.*]

MACMILLAN   I think of his wife. Of both of them. How they must be feeling tonight. What a torment. [*Pause.*] The press'll make their lives a misery. They should go away somewhere.

WIDDOWES   Mr Butler has arranged for a police guard to be posted outside Mr Profumo's house.

MACMILLAN   Good. Thank goodness I asked the Lord Chancellor to take action on this. [*to* RITCHIE] It was the last thing I did before I came away on holiday. I asked the Lord Chancellor to see if there was any substance in all these damn rumours that are flying about. [*to* WIDDOWES] Lucky I did that, Oliver.

WIDDOWES   Yes, sir, it was.

[MACMILLAN *looks at* RITCHIE, *suddenly realising that he does not know him.*]

MACMILLAN   Your name is what?

RITCHIE   Ritchie, sir,

MACMILLAN   Ritchie, yes. What exactly is your function? Are you on Mr Profumo's staff?

RITCHIE   MI5, sir.

MACMILLAN   MI5...?

WIDDOWES   There was some concern, if you remember, about the security aspect.

MACMILLAN   [*irritated.*] Yes, yes, of course I remember.

[*He glares at* RITCHIE.]

The importance of so-called security has been grossly exaggerated. This is not a police state. I have an aversion to all this prying and probing.

[*He returns the letter to* WIDDOWES.]

When was I first told about Profumo and the girl?

WIDDOWES   In February. While you were in Italy, the General Manager of a Sunday newspaper told us that Mr Profumo had compromised himself with a girl who was also having an affair with the Russian Naval Attaché, Captain Ivanov. We sent you a memorandum about this when you returned to London.

MACMILLAN   A tart. Calls herself a model. Trying to sell her story to the newspaper. Ludicrous. De Gaulle had just vetoed our entry into Europe. Unemployment figures were up. It was the coldest winter for years. And, if I remember rightly, we were fifteen points behind Labour in the Gallup Poll. I had more important things to worry about.

WIDDOWES   There was bound to be a degree of anxiety. The Minister of War was being linked with a Russian who was almost certainly an intelligence officer.

MACMILLAN   Yes, but Profumo denied it. Said he'd sue anyone who printed such a story. Isn't that right? Didn't he say that?

WIDDOWES   Yes.

MACMILLAN   Well, I believed him. We all believed him. Didn't he sue some French magazine?

WIDDOWES   *Paris-Match* and the Italian paper, *Il Tempo*.

MACMILLAN   Well, then — of course we believed him. What happened next?

WIDDOWES   The girl disappeared.

MACMILLAN   Disappeared...? I don't remember that.

WIDDOWES   She'd been called as a witness in the trial of a West Indian drug trafficker. She failed to turn up and Mr Wigg started making trouble.

MACMILLAN   Oh yes. Mr Wigg.

WIDDOWES   He suggested that she'd been spirited away in case she said something that might embarrass Mr Profumo. He also dropped a few dark hints about Captain Ivanov and what he called 'security considerations'.

MACMILLAN   [*to* RITCHIE] Do you know Mr Wigg? [*without waiting for a reply*] Dreadful man. Smug and self-righteous — like so many Labour Members of Parliament. You'd think he'd been appointed Keeper of the Public Morals.

WIDDOWES   Be that as it may, sir, he's remarkably well informed. He's got a dossier on everyone involved — Mr Profumo, the girl, Stephen Ward —

MACMILLAN   Who is this fellow Ward? I gather he claims to have met me.

WIDDOWES   He's an osteopath. Rather good, they say. He has rooms in Harley Street or Wigmore Street — and an extremely fashionable clientele. He's also something of an amateur artist. Does drawings of famous people for the *Illustrated London News*. That's how he met you. He came to the House of Commons and did a sketch.

MACMILLAN Of me?

WIDDOWES Yes.

MACMILLAN When was this?

WIDDOWES A couple of years ago.

MACMILLAN I don't remember.

WIDDOWES No reason why you should. He was only with you for half an hour or so.

MACMILLAN And this girl — the tart — she was living with him, is that right?

WIDDOWES Yes. He seems to know quite a number of pretty girls and arranges introductions, as it were, to various friends and associates.

MACMILLAN An amateur pimp as well as an amateur artist.

WIDDOWES Something of the sort. He provides girls for Lord Astor, and has a weekend cottage on the Astor estate. That's where Mr Profumo met the girl.

MACMILLAN [*to* RITCHIE] Amazing how people live, don't you think? All this promiscuity. I don't know how they find the time — or the energy. [*to* WIDDOWES] When did Profumo make his statement to the House?

WIDDOWES March the twenty-second. The Chief Whip and others thought Mr Profumo should make some sort of a reply to the innuendoes and rumours emanating from George Wigg. They prepared the text overnight and it was shown to you in the morning.

MACMILLAN Yes, it seemed clear and pretty convincing. A silly scrape, nothing more. [*to* RITCHIE] Profumo had written a note to the tart calling her 'darling'. That didn't seem particularly significant. Profumo and his wife move in theatrical, rather

raffish society. They call each other 'darling' all
the time. He'd been foolish, not wicked. Or so
it seemed to me. If I had any doubts about
Profumo's integrity, they were dispelled by his
statement. I couldn't believe he would perjure
himself in the courts and mislead the House of
Commons. How wrong I was.

WIDDOWES   You and many others.

MACMILLAN   I should've been more alert. When rumours per-
sist it usually means there's something keeping
them alive. And that something is quite often a
grain of truth.

> [*He is silent for a moment, considering the
> situation.*]

He lied to me, to his friends and to Parliament.
The press will have a field day. [*to* WIDDOWES]
When did he tell his wife?

WIDDOWES   It must've been the day before yesterday.

MACMILLAN   I thought they were going to Venice.

WIDDOWES   Yes, they went last Thursday for the Whitsun
weekend. They planned to come back tomorrow.
But then, as I understand it, the Lord Chancellor
telephoned Mr Profumo to change the time of
an appointment. He wanted to interview Mr
Profumo as part of the enquiry he's carrying out
on your instructions.

MACMILLAN   Yes, I see.

WIDDOWES   The phone call obviously scared Mr Profumo and
he decided to come clean. He told his wife over
dinner at the Danieli. They returned home immediately.

MACMILLAN   Dreadful. Poor woman. [*to* RITCHIE] Charming. Do you know her?

RITCHIE   No, sir, not personally.

MACMILLAN   An actress. Valerie something. Charming. Hobson.

WIDDOWES   Mr Profumo telephoned the Chief Whip. He came to the office and told us what had happened. He gave us his letter of resignation.

MACMILLAN   What a dreadful thing. A tragedy. This is the stuff of tragedy, Oliver. A fine and able man destroyed by a tart. The very stuff of tragedy.

WIDDOWES   The question is, sir, what do we do now?

[MACMILLAN *pauses for a moment.*]

MACMILLAN   My inclination is to say 'nothing'. Sit tight and let it blow over.

WIDDOWES   I don't think we can do that.

MACMILLAN   Why not? Heavens above, when Hugh Gaitskell was Leader of the Opposition he had a long affair with Ian Fleming's wife and nobody gave a damn.

WIDDOWES   Mr Gaitskell was not the Minister of War, nor is Mrs Fleming a tart.

RITCHIE   And she wasn't sleeping with a Russian spy at the same time.

[MACMILLAN *can think of no reasonable response to this; he changes tack.*]

MACMILLAN   You're both making far too much of this. I don't believe it'll become a major problem. What have we done wrong? Nothing. Profumo lied to us and we believed him. Is that reprehensible? Of course we believed him. He's a man of honour. Or so we thought. All we're guilty of is an excess of loyalty and trust.

WIDDOWES   I don't think the press will see it that way.

MACMILLAN   I don't give a damn about the press. They're petty, spiteful and ill-informed.

WIDDOWES   You don't think it might be a good idea if you went back to London?

MACMILLAN   No I do not. That would only serve to make things look more serious than they are. We have planned to play golf at Gleneagles and that is precisely what we shall do. Rab can take care of things in London. What's the point in having a Deputy Prime Minister if you don't let him deputise from time to time? Makes him feel useful. Which of course he is. Enormously. [*to* RITCHIE] Did you hear what happened when Rab went to Chequers to see Winston? It was during the war. Winston was lying in bed, smoking a Corona, surrounded by red boxes, and with a large black cat curled up on his feet. It was about eleven o'clock in the morning. "Look at this cat," said Winston, "this cat is doing more for the war effort than you are." — Rab was Minister of Education at the time — "This cat," said Winston, "is providing me with a hot-water bottle, thus saving the country fuel and power!" [*He laughs.*] Good old Rab. The only man in England who can serve six guests from a single partridge. [*He goes to the door.*] I'd better go and give McFee his clock. [*to* WIDDOWES] Do you remember McFee? Darling man. Seventy, looks forty. Remarkable.

RITCHIE   Just before you go, sir.

[MACMILLAN *pauses by the door.*]

There is something I think you should know.

MACMILLAN Oh?

RITCHIE A complication. Concerning the Russian, sir. Captain Ivanov.

MACMILLAN What about him?

RITCHIE It's not quite as straightforward as Mr Widdowes made it seem.

MACMILLAN What isn't?

RITCHIE The Security Service was interested in Captain Ivanov long before he was involved with Miss Keeler and Mr Profumo.

MACMILLAN Why was that?

RITCHIE We knew he was a spy.

MACMILLAN You *knew*...?

RITCHIE When Captain Ivanov came to London three years ago he was described as Assistant Naval Attaché at the Soviet Embassy. That's the accepted diplomatic cover for an intelligence officer. It's the same for our people in Moscow. Assistant Naval Attaché equals spy.

MACMILLAN I see.

RITCHIE Ivanov was trained by the GRU, Russian military intelligence. We knew that.

MACMILLAN Yes, I see.

RITCHIE He's also a member of the Soviet élite. His wife's the daughter of the chairman of the Supreme Court and his brother-in-law is a member of the GRU *rezidentura* at the London Embassy. It's these personal connections that made him particularly interesting as far as we were concerned.

MACMILLAN	Are Captain Ivanov and his family circle relevant to my playing golf?
RITCHIE	I think it's something you should be aware of, sir.

[MACMILLAN *sighs and sits in an armchair.*]

MACMILLAN	Very well. You'd better explain.
RITCHIE	Ivanov is a very social sort of man. Extrovert. Loud voice, laughs a lot, life and soul of the party, likes a drink —
MACMILLAN	Don't they all?
RITCHIE	— something of a ladies' man. He finds it hard to resist a pretty girl. It was because of this, sir, that he seemed an obvious target. It was decided that we would try to compromise him. Make him defect, you see. Or make him work for us.

[MACMILLAN, *now alert, turns to* WIDDOWES.]

MACMILLAN	Did you know about this?
WIDDOWES	No, sir.
MACMILLAN	[*to* RITCHIE] Was anyone in my office informed?
RITCHIE	I don't know, sir. I could find out, of course.
MACMILLAN	Please do. Go on.
RITCHIE	The plan was very simple. Find a girl to seduce Ivanov. Take photographs. Confront Ivanov with the evidence and suggest that we'd make things difficult for him if he didn't do what he was told.

[MACMILLAN *is angry. He rises to his feet.*]

MACMILLAN	Are you telling me that this plan was put into operation?
RITCHIE	Yes, sir.
MACMILLAN	Without informing me or my office?

RITCHIE I don't know who was informed, sir.

MACMILLAN [*to* WIDDOWES] Were we informed?

WIDDOWES I think not.

MACMILLAN [*to* RITCHIE] I disapprove very strongly of this sort of squalid enterprise. Any advantage or knowledge gained in this way is far outweighed by the moral damage done to our country. Your people know I disapprove. Such methods are distasteful to our national sentiment. I told Roger Hollis. I told Dick White. Which one do you work for?

RITCHIE Sir Roger, sir.

MACMILLAN I told him. He knows how I feel. Why wasn't I informed about this?

RITCHIE I don't know, sir.

MACMILLAN Of course you know. I was kept in the dark because Sir Roger knew I'd disapprove. He knew I'd put a stop to it.

RITCHIE We were hoping, sir, to gain some sort of credit with the American Intelligence community.

MACMILLAN What do you mean by that?

RITCHIE The CIA and Mr Hoover have a very low opinion of our Security Service. Burgess, Maclean, Philby, Vassall — it's been a succession of disasters — and there's a very real danger that the Americans will restrict the information they give us for fear that it'll go straight back to Moscow. I think the D-G spoke to you about this or sent you a briefing note.

MACMILLAN [*to* WIDDOWES] Did he?

WIDDOWES I'll check.

RITCHIE A success with Captain Ivanov would've helped

to revive their confidence in us — apart, of course, from being extremely useful in its own right.

[MACMILLAN *gives a grunt of grudging understanding.*]

MACMILLAN So what happened? How did you organise this entrapment?

RITCHIE We asked Stephen Ward to help us. He said he would provide a girl and introduce her to Ivanov.

WIDDOWES Why on earth did you choose a man like Ward?

RITCHIE Because of Lord Astor. As you know, sir, there are occasions when visiting Heads of State or other notables ask for female company. It's been our custom to ask Lord Astor to help us out in this respect. When we asked him about the Ivanov situation, he put us in touch with Stephen Ward.

MACMILLAN Is money involved? Did you make any payment to Ward?

RITCHIE Oh no, sir. He's a terrific social climber. Pretty girls are his passport into high society. He'll do anything to get on first name terms with a Duke or an Earl.

MACMILLAN He sounds a most objectionable creature.

WIDDOWES Actually he's quite charming.

MACMILLAN Have you met him?

WIDDOWES Smooth, perhaps, not charming. Yes, I met him at a dinner party.

MACMILLAN Whose dinner party?

WIDDOWES An artist called Vasco Lazzolo. He was painting Isobel's portrait.

MACMILLAN   That's the sort of circle he mixes in, is it? — artists and so forth?

RITCHIE   No, sir, he's more ambitious than that. He makes a point of cultivating anyone he thinks can give him a leg up socially: fashionable photographers, theatre people, politicians, Lord Astor, of course, the Marquess of Milford Haven, Prince Philip...

MACMILLAN   [*to* WIDDOWES] Is this true?

WIDDOWES   So I believe.

MACMILLAN   We don't want the Palace to get dragged into this.

RITCHIE   Prince Philip hasn't seen him for years.

MACMILLAN   That wouldn't stop the press making a scandal out of it. [*to* WIDDOWES] You'd better have a word with Commander Colville. The least we can do is to warn him. [*to* RITCHIE] Go on.

RITCHIE   Stephen Ward has a cottage at Cliveden, on Lord Astor's estate. He took Ivanov down for the weekend. The girl, Miss Keeler, was also there. Everything seemed to be working very well, but then, by chance, Mr Profumo bumped into Miss Keeler. Literally bumped into her. He and his wife were staying at the big house with Lord Astor. Miss Keeler was swimming in the pool. Without a bathing costume. Mr Profumo was very attracted to Miss Keeler and began an affair with her. My department soon became aware of this. It was all a bit of a joke really. Ivanov would be arriving for a rendezvous with Miss Keeler just as Mr Profumo was driving away in the War Office Humber.

> [RITCHIE *grins, but* MACMILLAN *and* WIDDOWES *are not amused.* RITCHIE *continues his narrative.*]

We told the Cabinet office what was going on and they warned Mr Profumo of the potential security risk. He stopped seeing the girl immediately.

MACMILLAN But all this happened ages ago. Surely? Didn't it? I seem to remember hearing gossip about the Cliveden weekend. When was it? Two years ago? Eighteen months?

RITCHIE Almost two years.

WIDDOWES July '61.

MACMILLAN So why has it become a problem now?

RITCHIE Miss Keeler had a quarrel with her latest boyfriend — a black man with a reputation for violence. He went to Ward's house and fired a pistol at the front door. The police were called. The press started sniffing around. Miss Keeler tried to sell her story to the *Sunday Pictorial*. There was a threat of legal action against the paper and the deal collapsed. But it was obvious that the scandal was bound to break sooner or later. Ward's so-called friends began to give him the cold shoulder. His clients cancelled appointments. Lord Astor asked him to vacate the cottage at Cliveden. Then Miss Keeler's black boyfriend came up for trial at the Old Bailey. That's when she disappeared and ran away to Spain. Ward realised that his entire life was about to disintegrate. He made contact with us and tried putting on the pressure.

MACMILLAN What sort of pressure?

RITCHIE Implying that he'd spill the beans if we didn't help him.

MACMILLAN Blackmail.

RITCHIE   Of a sort.

MACMILLAN   Do you think he would spill the beans?

RITCHIE   It's possible. He's a loose cannon, unpredictable, and therefore dangerous. He's already been telling people that Mr Profumo and Miss Keeler were lovers; if he starts talking about his participation in the Ivanov thing, he could do the Service a lot of harm.

MACMILLAN   To say nothing of the damage he'd do to the Government.

WIDDOWES   Where is Ivanov? What's happened to him?

RITCHIE   Back in Moscow.

MACMILLAN   What do you intend to do about Ward?

RITCHIE   We've had discussions with the police and the Home Office. The immediate aim is to find a way to discredit anything he might say or any claims he might make.

MACMILLAN   How can you do that?

RITCHIE   Someone suggested prosecuting him under the Official Secrets Act.

WIDDOWES   Prosecuting him for what?

RITCHIE   There's a story going around that Ward asked Miss Keeler to ask Mr Profumo about the deployment of nuclear warheads in Germany.

WIDDOWES   My God.

MACMILLAN   Total nonsense, according to Roger Hollis.

WIDDOWES   Where did this story come from?

RITCHIE   Miss Keeler.

MACMILLAN   Sir Roger told me a few days ago. My first reaction was one of extreme alarm. It's the main reason I asked the Lord Chancellor to conduct an enquiry. But Sir Roger assures me there's nothing to worry about.

RITCHIE   It certainly wouldn't stand up in a Court of Law.

WIDDOWES   [*to* RITCHIE] Do you think Ward is a spy?

RITCHIE   No, no, most unlikely.

MACMILLAN   [*to* RITCHIE] You say he's putting on the pressure. What do you mean by that? What does he hope to achieve?

RITCHIE   He wants us to admit that we employed him in the Ivanov business. That, of course, we cannot do without revealing the whole plan — and, by so doing, admitting its failure.

MACMILLAN   So what's to be done? I will not allow the Government to be brought down by a tart.

RITCHIE   A charge of living off immoral earnings has also been suggested.

MACMILLAN   Might that work?

WIDDOWES   Ward's not a pimp.

RITCHIE   The police think they could get a conviction.

MACMILLAN   Is this being pursued?

RITCHIE   It is.

MACMILLAN   Very good.

WIDDOWES   Be careful. Ward may be immoral but he's not a criminal.

RITCHIE   He might be.

MACMILLAN   Is there any substantial proof against him? The Prosecution'll need more than Smoking Room gossip.

RITCHIE   The CID are investigating. I'm sure something'll be found.

MACMILLAN   Tell your office to keep me informed.

RITCHIE   Yes, sir.

MACMILLAN   Good. [*He goes to the door.*] I think it's inappropriate for me to discuss these matters any further. Government shouldn't be concerned with police procedure. I'll go and give McFee his clock. [*to* WIDDOWES] Are you coming?

WIDDOWES   I think I'll stay and talk things over with Mr Ritchie.

MACMILLAN   As you wish. Any other news from London?

WIDDOWES   Nothing urgent. Your daughter rang and left a message.

MACMILLAN   Which daughter?

WIDDOWES   Sarah. She's staying in Geneva a little longer than originally planned. She said she'd write to you.

MACMILLAN   Good. [*to* RITCHIE] Thank you for explaining things so clearly. I'm grateful.

[MACMILLAN *goes out.*]

[*A moment of silence.*]

RITCHIE   I need another drink. [*He goes to the drinks table.*] How about you?

WIDDOWES   No, thanks.

[*He watches as* RITCHIE *pours himself another Scotch.*]

Why weren't we told about this?

[RITCHIE *shrugs.*]

RITCHIE   No idea.

[WIDDOWES *bristles crossly.*]

WIDDOWES   What do you mean, no idea...?

RITCHIE   I'm just a messenger boy.

WIDDOWES   Your department clearly knew everything — and
            has known it for months, years.

> [RITCHIE *remains silent, holding his Scotch, look-
> ing at* WIDDOWES.]

            The plan to compromise Ivanov. Stephen Ward's
            role in all that. The story about him asking Miss
            Keeler about nuclear weapons. Mr Profumo's
            adultery. You knew everything.

RITCHIE   Yes, I suppose that's true.

WIDDOWES   And you don't think the Prime Minister should've
            been told?

RITCHIE   Sex is a forbidden subject as far as the PM is con-
            cerned. You know that as well as I do. And we
            all know why.

WIDDOWES   That's not the point.

RITCHIE   Anyway it's not our job to report on the moral
            behaviour of government ministers. What they
            do between the sheets is their own business.

WIDDOWES   Not when national security is at risk.

RITCHIE   But it wasn't. We knew it wasn't.

WIDDOWES   Even so, the Government should've been informed.

RITCHIE   I'm pretty sure the D-G had a meeting with the
            Home Secretary.

WIDDOWES   What about the Prime Minister?

RITCHIE   We were satisfied there was no security problem.
            The matter was closed. Why bother the Prime
            Minister?

> [*Pause.* WIDDOWES *fumes silently.*]

Do you think it'd be all right if I used the phone?

WIDDOWES   I suppose so.

RITCHIE   I told my wife I'd be back by late afternoon. Obviously that is not the case. [*He dials a number.*] Yes, could I have Beckenham 5832, please? Beckenham in Kent. 5832. Thank you.

> [*There is a pause while the call is connected.* RITCHIE *sips his Scotch.*]

What's his daughter doing in Geneva? Drying out again? Must be difficult for him, bloody painful — having children who are alcoholics — he's bound to blame himself, don't you think? — bound to.

> [*The call is answered.*]

Hullo? — Maureen, it's me — Yes, all right, not bad — Look, I'm not going to get back until tomorrow evening — No, no, later than that. It'll be too late for the theatre, so you'd better ring the Old Vic and see if you can change the tickets —OK — Yes, OK — All right, take care, see you tomorrow. [*He hangs up.*] Bloody nuisance. We booked ages ago: *Peer Gynt.* It comes off soon. [*He sits. Pause.*] Amazing, really, meeting him like that. The Prime Minister. Like seeing a film star in the street. I once saw Robert Mitchum in Leicester Square. I smiled and said hullo, I knew it was a familiar face, but couldn't think who it was, then I thought, my God, it's Robert Mitchum. [*He chuckles. Pause.*] It must be odd to be such a public figure. The Prime Minister must be recognised everywhere. I mean, everywhere he goes, people stop and stare. Do you think he enjoys it?

WIDDOWES   I've no idea.

RITCHIE   He probably does. He is a bit of an actor, after all.
             Don't you think? All this unflappable Edwardian
             grandee stuff. [*imitation*] "You've never had it
             so good." [*normal voice*] All a bit of a perform-
             ance. A very good performance, very skilled, very
             engaging, but a performance nonetheless. Un-
             like her, of course — she's the genuine article,
             anyone can see that.

             [WIDDOWES *does not want to pursue this line of*
             conversation. He startles RITCHIE *with an*
             unexpected question.]

WIDDOWES   Tell me the truth. Is something going on?

RITCHIE   Going on? What do you mean?

WIDDOWES   Was it deliberate policy that the Prime Minister
             should not be briefed?

RITCHIE   Of course not. Why should it be?

WIDDOWES   You tell me.

RITCHIE   Look, I've explained — there was no security risk.
             Stephen Ward is not a spy.

WIDDOWES   What about your plan to blackmail Ivanov?

RITCHIE   Not *my* plan.

WIDDOWES   It's customary, as you know, to brief both the
             Home Secretary and the Prime Minister's office
             about something as sensitive as that. It's com-
             mon procedure. Why wasn't it observed?

             [RITCHIE *hesitates.*]

RITCHIE   The PM gave my boss a bloody hard time over
             the Vassall affair and Sir Roger had no wish to be
             hauled over the coals for something that was
             aborted before it even got off the ground. Since

there had been no breach of security, it seemed best to keep mum. Least said, soonest mended.

[WIDDOWES *suspects there is more; he waits.*]

Also — between ourselves — there's been a certain amount of internal wrangling.

WIDDOWES Between whom?

RITCHIE About Stephen Ward. Between those who thought it was a good idea to use his services and those who thought he was too left-wing and unreliable. When things started to unravel, the D-G decided to take the lowest of low profiles.

WIDDOWES In other words, the PM wasn't told because Sir Roger was covering up a general disarray within MI5.

RITCHIE I wouldn't put it like that.

WIDDOWES I'm sure you wouldn't.

RITCHIE Look, does it matter? No great harm has been done.

WIDDOWES MI5 is not a self-ruling secret police force. The Prime Minister should've been informed.

[RITCHIE *tries to lighten the atmosphere with an ill-judged joke.*]

RITCHIE You know what they say. Politicians come and go. We go on for ever.

[WIDDOWES *grunts with irritation and pours himself another gin.* RITCHIE *starts opening cupboard doors.*]

WIDDOWES What are you looking for?

RITCHIE Something to eat. I'm starving.

WIDDOWES Ask Mrs Brennan.

RITCHIE   She'll be over in the barn watching old What's-it getting his clock.

WIDDOWES   Teapot.

RITCHIE   What?

WIDDOWES   It's a teapot, not a clock.

            [*Pause.* WIDDOWES *sips his gin and tonic.* RITCHIE *glances at him.*]

RITCHIE   Don't take it personally.

            [WIDDOWES *glares angrily.*]

WIDDOWES   Don't take *what* personally?

            [RITCHIE *is anxious to avoid an argument.*]

RITCHIE   Nothing. Not important.

            [WIDDOWES, *on the other hand, decides to attack.*]

WIDDOWES   I suppose what I find offensive — personally — is the assumption that because he's the sort of man he is — that's to say, of a certain age, of a certain class — the Prime Minister is unable to grasp the complexities of the rather grubby world that you inhabit.

RITCHIE   I didn't say that.

WIDDOWES   You implied it.

RITCHIE   I was only trying to explain, as clearly as I could, a difficult and rather delicate situation.

WIDDOWES   It was the underlying tone of condescension I found particularly offensive. Personally. The unspoken but clearly expressed opinion that he's a man in decline, outdated, redundant.

RITCHIE   Well perhaps he is. Outdated. Not that he can do much about that. Happens to us all eventually.

[WIDDOWES *ignores this.*]

WIDDOWES For what it's worth, and I certainly don't expect you to agree, I believe the PM to be a man of principle. He represents certain values that I, for one, will be sad to see disappear — as they're bound to, I'm afraid, when the faceless entrepreneurs take over. Words like honour spring to mind — I'm sure your lip is curling — integrity, respect, probity —values we dismiss at our peril.

[RITCHIE *is sipping his Scotch. Pause.*]

RITCHIE What about firing Selwyn Lloyd? Was that an honourable thing to do?

WIDDOWES Selwyn was not a first-rate Chancellor. The economy was going downhill. Something had to be done.

RITCHIE I'm not talking about why — how.

WIDDOWES There's never an easy way to do these things.

RITCHIE Poor bugger. Foreign Secretary, then Chancellor — how long had he been in the Government? Nine years? Ten? Not much of a reward to find out you've been sacked by reading about it in the *Daily Mail*.

WIDDOWES It wasn't like that.

RITCHIE You're going to tell me Mr Butler was to blame.

WIDDOWES And so he was. He had lunch with the owner of the *Daily Mail*. He blabbed. The *Mail* printed the story. It was entirely Rab's fault. He's hopelessly indiscreet.

RITCHIE On the other hand, of course, the PM might've behaved like a shit because it was the necessary thing to do. Perhaps Machiavelli was right all along.

WIDDOWES   What's he got to do with it?

RITCHIE   He said the moral standards appropriate in private life would almost certainly be wrong — even damaging — in public matters, where one needs a certain amount of deceit, treachery, and guile.

WIDDOWES   That's just cynical posturing.

RITCHIE   Is it?

WIDDOWES   Trying to defend the indefensible.

RITCHIE   You don't think the Prime Minister would agree?

WIDDOWES   I'm quite sure he wouldn't.

RITCHIE   Let me tell you something. A couple of years ago Roy Welensky came to London for a conference on the future of the Central African Federation. He stayed at the Hyde Park Hotel. We bugged his rooms. The authorisation came from the Home Secretary. So don't tell me the Prime Minister didn't know what was going on.

WIDDOWES   Welensky is a dangerous man. Headstrong and aggressive.

RITCHIE   He's also the Prime Minister of a Commonwealth country, so presumably he felt he could trust the British Government not to stick an SF on his phone.

WIDDOWES   The situation in Northern Rhodesia was on a knife edge. The PM was genuinely afraid there might be a blood bath.

RITCHIE   Yes, I'm sure there's always a good reason. [*He goes to the telephone.*] Excuse me a moment. Something I forgot. [*He dials a number.*] Yes, could I have Beckenham 5832, please? Beckenham in Kent. 5832. Thank you.

[*A pause while the call is connected.*]

Actually, I find it reassuring that the PM behaved as he did. I'd rather have someone like Machiavelli running the country than a shambling old snob who's only at home on the grouse moor. Perhaps an unexpectedly ruthless heart beats beneath that Old Etonian tie. What d'you think? Is the role of poseur itself a pose?

[*The call is answered.*]

Maureen, it's me again — Listen, I was thinking, you'd better ring Andrew and Liz. I said we'd meet them at the theatre. You'd better explain what's happened. Either they can go tomorrow by themselves or we can all try for tickets next week — OK, fine. See you tomorrow.

[*He hangs up.*]

WIDDOWES   So what's going to happen?

RITCHIE   In what respect?

WIDDOWES   About Stephen Ward. I don't like this idea of a criminal prosecution. It's not right.

RITCHIE   I don't think we need waste much sympathy on Stephen Ward. A middle-aged wanker with ideas above his station.

WIDDOWES   The whole thing could so easily backfire. It'd only need one person — Lord Astor — to stand up and say "This man is not a pimp" and the whole case would collapse.

RITCHIE   Yes, but he won't will he? None of them will.

WIDDOWES   'Them' being...?

RITCHIE   What my chief calls the Ward *galère*. 'Them'. What journalists call the Establishment. Whatever that may mean. [*He sips his Scotch.*] It's a very shallow concept, don't you think? The Establishment. It implies that it's just a question of going to the right school or knowing the right people. Very glib. William Cobbett had a much better idea. Did you ever read Cobbett? He had the idea that Britain was controlled by what he called 'The Thing' — a ruthless and invisible power that spreads its influence throughout the whole of the country's political and social life. 'The Thing' is utterly selfish — it exists for itself and for the people who support and succour it: the men and women who are both its slaves and its beneficiaries. Bankers, working-class novelists, stockbrokers, Hampstead socialists, readers of the *Spectator*. They know if they conform to its requirements, 'The Thing' will keep them safe and well fed. Members of the Establishment, so-called, are predominately right-wing. 'The Thing', on the other hand, is more powerful than party politics — it exerts its irresistible charm on both left and right. And it's stronger now than it was in Cobbett's time, because 'The Thing' is organic: it learns and it grows. It also cuts our balls off — or rather, it encourages us to cut our own balls off in the hope of a reward — an appointment to a prestigious board, say, drinks at Downing Street, an OBE, an invitation to the Royal Academy Dinner.

WIDDOWES   It's all very well for you to sneer — you're part of it too.

RITCHIE   Of course I am, and very pleased to be so. That's the cunning of it. Whether we admit to it or not, we all want to be part of 'The Thing'. We all want to be on the inside, smiling smugly at the poor sods who haven't made it. I mean, take a man like David Frost — (—he's the perfect example of what I'm talking about.)

[MACMILLAN *enters and interrupts him.*]

MACMILLAN It wasn't a clock, at all — McFee's present. It was a teapot. I felt such a fool. I said a few words, then I said how pleased I was to present him with this fine clock, only to find it was a teapot.

[WIDDOWES *and* RITCHIE *respond with polite smiles.* MACMILLAN *sits.*]

So — you've been talking. What are your conclusions? What are your thoughts?

RITCHIE There wasn't much to talk about. Mr Profumo did not tell the truth. That's the beginning and the end of it.

MACMILLAN It may be the beginning, Mr Ritchie, but I very much fear it will not be the end.

[RITCHIE *realises that this is a reprimand. There is a moment of uneasy silence.*]

When I was at the Foreign Office, my Principal Private Secretary was a charming man called Patrick Hancock. He finds it absolutely necessary to tell the truth, no matter how difficult or painful it might be. While he was at Winchester, he'd been bullied mercilessly by one of the older boys. This boy, knowing Hancock suffered from claustrophobia, would push him into a tuck-box and sit on the lid. Hancock suffered dreadfully. Many years later, forty or so years later, Hancock received a letter from the bully, who had subsequently become a clergyman and was now ill and dying. He bitterly regretted his boyhood cruelties and begged Hancock to forgive him. Hancock spent a sleepless night trying to decide how to respond compassionately and yet truthfully. In the morning, he sent a telegram. "Regret cannot forgive. Hancock."

> [RITCHIE *laughs rather self-consciously;* WIDDOWES, *having heard the story before, merely smiles.*]

Would you mind leaving us for a few minutes? I need to talk to Oliver.

RITCHIE   Yes, sir, of course.

MACMILLAN   You must be hungry.

RITCHIE   Yes, I am.

MACMILLAN   Go and find Mrs Brennan; she'll get you something to eat.

> [RITCHIE *exits.*]

> [*There is a moment of silence before* MACMILLAN *speaks.*]

I was thinking — if the police do decide to bring a case against Ward, the timing will be very important. For us, I mean. For the Government.

WIDDOWES   In what way?

MACMILLAN   I would like the Lord Chancellor's report to be made public before Ward is charged.

WIDDOWES   Surely the timing is up to the police?

MACMILLAN   Of course.

WIDDOWES   I don't think we can do much about that.

MACMILLAN   My point is — it would be very advantageous if the public could see that the police were taking action because of the Government's initiative, and not the other way round. You see what I mean?

WIDDOWES Yes, but the Lord Chancellor has hardly started his investigations.

MACMILLAN I told him to work with all speed.

WIDDOWES Even so.

MACMILLAN I told him to keep it in the family. "Talk to the police, ministers, civil servants," I said, "keep it in the family." That should make his task much easier, don't you think? And therefore one might reasonably expect his report within a couple of weeks or so. Wouldn't you say?

WIDDOWES Possibly, I suppose. Perhaps.

MACMILLAN If Ward is charged with living off immoral earnings, Jack Profumo might well be called as a witness. The adverse publicity would be overwhelming. We need to show the public that we weren't just sitting around twiddling our thumbs.

WIDDOWES Yes, sir — yes, I understand what you're saying.

MACMILLAN Therefore, if the police can delay their action until the Lord Chancellor's report is made public, it'd be extremely useful.

WIDDOWES We can't ask the police to postpone — to deliberately postpone — any action they might want to take against Ward.

MACMILLAN No, no, of course not, I'm not suggesting anything of the sort. [*Briefest pause.*] Even so, you might like to have a few words with the Commissioner. See what his plans are. Make him aware of our concern. Will you do that, Oliver?

[WIDDOWES *is uneasy. He nods his agreement.*]

WIDDOWES   Yes, sir, I'll do what I can.

MACMILLAN   Good. Thank you. [*Pause.*] You see, the point is,
            I feel — to some extent — responsible for what
            has happened.

            [WIDDOWES *is astonished.*]

WIDDOWES   Responsible...? How?

MACMILLAN   To some extent.

WIDDOWES   But why?

            [MACMILLAN *merely shrugs.*]

            You didn't know about Stephen Ward or the
            Russian. MI5 hadn't briefed you. You didn't know
            anything. How could you be responsible?

MACMILLAN   I mean later. Subsequent events could've been
            handled differently.

WIDDOWES   In what way?

MACMILLAN   I should've done it myself. I shouldn't have left it
            to other people.

WIDDOWES   Left what?

MACMILLAN   I asked Selwyn to talk to him. I'd heard all these
            stories about Profumo and the girl. At first, I
            didn't believe a word of it. It seemed so unlikely
            — I mean, there he was, charming wife, family,
            career, everything a man could wish for, I
            couldn't believe he'd throw it all away just to sleep
            with a tart. But then — well, the rumours seemed
            too widespread to dismiss completely. So I asked
            Selwyn to go and talk to him. They're old friends.
            "Find out," I said. "Ask him. Be blunt." So they
            talked. Profumo lied. Selwyn believed him com-
            pletely. [*Pause.*] If I'd spoken to Profumo, if I had
            asked him directly, I'm sure he'd have told me

the truth. And then, of course, things would've been very different. We could've found a way out.

WIDDOWES   It's pointless wondering what might or might not have happened — and it's certainly pointless blaming yourself.

[MACMILLAN *pays no attention.*]

MACMILLAN   It's not the sexual thing, it's lying to Parliament. Therein lies the real damage. Heavens above, Profumo's trangression was not exactly uncommon. Hundreds of men do it every day. Thousands. Gladstone said he'd known eleven Prime Ministers, and seven of them were adulterers. Look at Jack Kennedy. Girls all over the place. The point is — if Profumo had told the truth and issued a public statement, none of this would've happened. He'd have been in disgrace, of course, he'd have had to resign as a Minister, but he could've stayed on as an MP, he wouldn't have been ruined. You know what Trollope said: "If you own up in a genial sort of way, the House of Commons will forgive anything." He was right. It's true.

[*He prompts a response from* WIDDOWES.]

Isn't that right?

WIDDOWES   Yes, sir.

MACMILLAN   Isn't that true?

WIDDOWES   Yes, sir, it is.

MACMILLAN   I should've spoken to him, but I didn't. I couldn't. I should've been frank and direct with him. But I wasn't.

[*He looks at* WIDDOWES.]

I found the whole thing too difficult, Too difficult and too painful. I think you understand why.

[WIDDOWES *nods. Pause.* MACMILLAN *rises to his feet with a sigh.*]

What a mess it all is. A pretty kettle of fish, as one used to say — though heaven knows why; a totally meaningless phrase, I've always thought. [*He goes to the drinks table.*] Would you like a drink?

WIDDOWES   No, thank you, sir.

[MACMILLAN *pours himself a brandy and soda.*]

MACMILLAN   I made rather a good speech just now. With Jack Profumo very much in mind, I extolled the virtues of Christian ethics and moral rectitude. McFee wept. It was very touching. [*He sits and sips his brandy.*] I don't understand how anyone can arrive at a sound moral judgement without religion. Obviously many people do. Most people, I daresay, since we live in a secular age. How is it possible?

WIDDOWES   I suppose there must be some sort of innate impulse to do right and to abhor wrong. Otherwise mankind wouldn't survive.

MACMILLAN   You're right, it wouldn't. But it must be more than just an innate impulse, don't you think? Society requires a shared morality. Certain prohibitions have to be observed. You can't have people driving the wrong way down a one-way street. And in my view — flawed and antiquated though it may be — morals and religion are inextricably entwined. One needs the moral authority one gets from the Church, otherwise you'll end up with the godless free-for-all that so many progressive thinkers seem to advocate.

WIDDOWES You could argue that morality is, or should be, a matter of individual judgement.

MACMILLAN So it is — up to a point. But we are, after all, a community. We have to live together under the same roof. And if you want to share the house, you have to accept the rules of the family. It's like playing snakes-and-ladders. The point of the game is not observing the rules, but without observing the rules, the game is impossible.

WIDDOWES Yes, but who makes the rules? Who's head of the family?

MACMILLAN God, if you're a believer.

WIDDOWES And if you're not...?

MACMILLAN That's what I'm asking you. How can one arrive at a sound moral judgement without religion?

WIDDOWES I don't think morality should necessarily be imposed upon us by some supernatural force. It's to do with other people, surely? — an awareness of other people. Moral standards are, or should be, the standards of conduct of which a reasonable man reasonably approves.

MACMILLAN Decency, in other words.

WIDDOWES Decency, the protection of our preferred way of life, the avoidance of pain, open-mindedness, honesty, compassion.

[MACMILLAN *looks at him.*]

MACMILLAN The avoidance of pain.

WIDDOWES Amongst other things.

MACMILLAN Giving or receiving?

WIDDOWES   I meant giving. It could, I suppose, be either.

MACMILLAN Yes. [*He takes a sip of brandy.*] Did Mr Ritchie say anything more about the Profumo situation?

WIDDOWES   Nothing of any importance. He said there'd been some internal arguments about the wisdom of employing Stephen Ward.

MACMILLAN Good, I'm glad to hear it. At least it shows there are some people in the Security Service with a modicum of common sense. [*Brief pause.*] He seems rather bright. Ritchie.

WIDDOWES   Yes, I think he is. I don't like him much, but he's certainly no fool.

           [MACMILLAN *sips his brandy.*]

MACMILLAN Dorothy thinks it's all a Russian plot. She may be right.

WIDDOWES   What does she mean? What sort of plot?

MACMILLAN A conspiracy to drive me from office. Create a scandal. The Government falls. Labour forms a new administration. Stranger things have happened.

WIDDOWES   I don't think it's very likely.

MACMILLAN Maybe not. [*Pause.*] Dear Dorothy. She said a few words at the presentation. They all adored her. You could feel the warmth. She treats everyone the same, you see, it doesn't matter who they are: a grouse keeper, a gardener, de Gaulle. She still gets Christmas cards from the working people we knew in Stockton thirty years ago. I don't know what I'd do without her. [*Pause.*] The estate manager is as drunk as an owl. That tall fellow with a squint. Completely fuddled. Three sheets in the wind. When he saw me, he tried to pretend he was sober. Enormously comic. There's something enormously comic about a drunken man trying to gather unto himself the tattered remnants of his dignity. [*He chuckles.*] Did you ever hear Bob Boothby's story about the tipsy butler? It was some time in the thirties. Twenties or thirties. He was very sought-after socially. Bob. Good-looking, dashing, unmarried. He was always getting asked to the best houses. On this occasion he was having dinner with one of the famous hostesses of the time. Emerald Cunard, perhaps, or it may've been Sybil Colefax. Anyway, whoever it was had a butler of whom she was particularly fond. The trouble was, he was always drinking too much and used to arrive in the dining room as tight as a tick. So there they all were, settling down at the table. Soup was being served. It was a big party. Austen Chamberlain was one of the guests. He must've been Foreign Secretary at the time. In comes the butler, drunk and reeling. The hostess — it was Mrs Greville, not Lady Cunard, it was Mrs Ronnie Greville — she wrote a note and gave it to the butler. The note said, "You are drunk. Leave the room immediately." So the butler took the note and read it very carefully. Then he walked around the table and gave the note to Austen Chamberlain. A priceless moment. Chamberlain was so astonished his eye-glass fell out.

[WIDDOWES *laughs.*]

One used to come across drunken servants far more frequently in the old days than one does now. I suppose their living conditions have improved somewhat.

WIDDOWES   Fewer people have servants.

MACMILLAN   True. Diana Cooper had a drunken cook. Do you
            know Diana? One of my very dearest friends. A
            great beauty. Duff, her husband, got into Parlia-
            ment at the same time as I did. That was in the
            landslide victory of 1924. Duff at Oldham, me at
            Stockton. We both lost our seats five years later,
            when Stanley Baldwin was kicked out by the
            Labour Party — and deservedly so. He was a
            brave and honourable politician. Duff. The only
            Minister to resign over Munich. He was bitterly
            opposed to appeasement. After the war, he be-
            came our Ambassador in Paris. He died on a
            cruise ship on New Year's Eve. 1954. Up in the
            ballroom, they were singing and dancing and
            drinking champagne. Down in his cabin, Duff
            had a haemorrhage and died. A good man. What
            was I saying?

WIDDOWES   Drunken servants.

MACMILLAN   Ah yes. We'd been to some sort of literary party,
            Diana, Bobbety Salisbury, Dorothy and me —we
            were going to have dinner with Diana at her
            house in Maida Vale — this was about a couple
            of years ago — but when we got there, Diana
            found her new cook drunk and senseless, lying
            on the kitchen floor. Food, of course, was ruined.
            So we all went to dinner to a restaurant in the
            Edgware Road. Rather good. The Angus Steak
            House. Have you come across it?

WIDDOWES   There are a number of Angus Steak Houses.

MACMILLAN   A number...? What do you mean?

WIDDOWES   It's a chain of restaurants. There are Angus Steak
            Houses throughout the country.

MACMILLAN   Really? I never go to restaurants. If I'm not at home, I dine at the club. I haven't been to a restaurant for years. But I was most impressed by the Angus Steak House. It seemed remarkable that ordinary men and women can just walk off the Edgware Road and order themselves a first-class meal. Diana thought the wine list was disappointing, but you can't have everything. [*Pause.*] I wonder if the Profumos' marriage will survive.

WIDDOWES   It'll be difficult for them.

MACMILLAN   Agonisingly difficult. One is always so touched by other people's unhappiness. [*He sips his brandy.*] I remember when Selwyn came to see me and told me he was going to be divorced. He looked so harassed and bedraggled. You know Selwyn. You know how tidy and immaculate he always is; not a hair out of place. I was quite shocked by his appearance. He offered to resign in case his divorce caused political embarrassment. He has a great sense of honour. Poor Selwyn. He's content, I think, being second-rate. But the failure of his marriage caused him much distress. She, of course, was a good bit younger than him. That was the root of the problem, or so I believe, so I was told.

                    [MRS BRENNAN *comes in.*]

              Yes, Mrs Brennan?

MRS BRENNAN   I've made the other gentleman a light supper, sir. I was wondering if Mr Widdowes would like something to eat.

WIDDOWES   No, thank you, Mrs Brennan. You're very kind.

                    [MACMILLAN *turns to* WIDDOWES.]

MACMILLAN   Have you had dinner?

WIDDOWES   It's all right, sir. I'm not hungry.

MACMILLAN   You ought to have something. [*to* MRS BRENNAN] Is there any cold chicken or ham?

MRS BRENNAN   There's the poached salmon, sir.

MACMILLAN   Is that what we had?

MRS BRENNAN   Yes, sir.

MACMILLAN   It was excellent. Do have some, Oliver.

WIDDOWES   What will you do, sir? Will you go back to the party?

MACMILLAN   I might. I might stay here and think things over. Don't worry about me, I'm perfectly happy. Come back and have a nightcap.

WIDDOWES   Yes, sir, I will.

[MRS BRENNAN *and* WIDDOWES *exit. The door closes.*]

[MACMILLAN *walks to the window and looks out at the darkening sky.*]

[*The flashback or memory is heralded by a glow of sunlight. The door opens and* LADY DOROTHY *enters. She looks much younger and is wearing clothes appropriate for the late 1920s.*]

LADY DOROTHY   Harold — what a surprise.

MACMILLAN   Hullo, Dorothy.

LADY DOROTHY   I thought you'd be at the club. Aren't you dining with Duff?

MACMILLAN   He telephoned. He's not feeling well.

LADY DOROTHY   What's the matter with him?

MACMILLAN   He keeps having dizzy spells. He was walking across St James's Park and he almost fainted. Most unpleasant.

LADY DOROTHY	Poor Duff. He's probably exhausted.
MACMILLAN	You think so?
LADY DOROTHY	You both are. All those weeks of electioneering. How many speeches did you make? I lost count. All the strain and anxiety. And then to lose. If you'd won, you'd both be full of beans.
MACMILLAN	Yes, maybe.
LADY DOROTHY	He needs a holiday. They should go to that place they liked so much. Where was it? Somewhere on Lake Garda. Diana said it was full of lemons and oleanders.
MACMILLAN	San Vigilio.
LADY DOROTHY	That's right. How clever of you to remember.
MACMILLAN	They can't get away now. Duff's writing his book on Talleyrand.
LADY DOROTHY	On who?
MACMILLAN	Talleyrand. French diplomat. Napoleon's Foreign Minister. And Diana's pregnant, so they're both pretty busy.
LADY DOROTHY	Diana's pregnant...?
MACMILLAN	So he said.
LADY DOROTHY	When's the baby due?
MACMILLAN	I've no idea.
LADY DOROTHY	Didn't he say? Didn't you ask?
MACMILLAN	Fairly soon, I think. In the autumn. He didn't say much about it. He was full of some wretched article in the *Saturday Review*. Virtually blaming the two of us for losing the election. "Socialists in disguise" they called us. Poor Duff. He was very upset. I told him to ignore it. We've nothing to

reproach ourselves for. The Party's stale and tired. If anyone's to blame, it's Stanley Baldwin. He's lost the will to govern. How can a man like that hope to win an election?

LADY DOROTHY   Harold. There's something I must tell you.

[*Her tone of voice surprises* MACMILLAN. *He turns towards her.*]

I've just been to see the doctor. Diana's not the only one who's pregnant.

[MACMILLAN *is astonished.*]

MACMILLAN   Dorothy. My dear.

[*Delighted, he goes to her. She evades his embrace.*]

LADY DOROTHY   No — please. Don't do that.

[MACMILLAN *freezes, his arms still extended in a proffered embrace.*]

It may not be yours.

[*He stands staring at her.*]

MACMILLAN   What...?

[*She turns away from him, deliberately avoiding his gaze.*]

What do you mean? I don't understand.

LADY DOROTHY   Don't be crass, Harold. Of course you understand.

MACMILLAN   If it's not mine, then — then, who...?

LADY DOROTHY   Bob, it's Bob's.

MACMILLAN   Bob...? Bob Boothby?

LADY DOROTHY   How many other Bobs do we know?

[MACMILLAN *is silent for a moment, trying to collect his racing thoughts.*]

MACMILLAN   When did it happen?

LADY DOROTHY   What do you mean?

MACMILLAN   When did you sleep with him?

LADY DOROTHY   We've been lovers for months.

END OF ACT ONE

ACT TWO

Everything is as it was at the end of Act One. The action is continuous.

MACMILLAN   When did it happen?

LADY DOROTHY   What do you mean?

MACMILLAN   When did you sleep with him?

LADY DOROTHY   We've been lovers for months.

> [MACMILLAN *utters a little gasp, as if the air had been driven out of his lungs.*]

I should've told you long ago. I wanted to. Bob said no. You were both so busy with the election. Wait till it's over, he said.

> [*Pause.*]

MACMILLAN   How did it begin?

LADY DOROTHY   Does it matter?

MACMILLAN   I want to know.

LADY DOROTHY   Perhaps it's better if you don't.

MACMILLAN   Tell me.

> [LADY DOROTHY *thinks for a moment and then decides to tell him what happened.*]

LADY DOROTHY   He took me to lunch.

MACMILLAN   When?

LADY DOROTHY   February.

MACMILLAN   He took you to lunch...? To a restaurant?

LADY DOROTHY   Well of course.

MACMILLAN   But what happened? Did he invite you? Did you meet by chance?

LADY DOROTHY   He telephoned.

MACMILLAN   And said what?

LADY DOROTHY   Would I like to have lunch.

MACMILLAN   Just you — not both of us?

LADY DOROTHY   You were away. In Stockton.

MACMILLAN   What did you say?

LADY DOROTHY   Yes, I said yes.

MACMILLAN   Why?

LADY DOROTHY   He's good company.

MACMILLAN   Did you tell him I was in Stockton?

LADY DOROTHY   He knew. He made a joke about it.

MACMILLAN   What did he say?

LADY DOROTHY   He said it's a good job your constituency is so far away from London.

MACMILLAN   So it was deliberate — he deliberately telephoned when I was in Stockton?

LADY DOROTHY   Yes.

MACMILLAN   Weren't you surprised?

LADY DOROTHY   Not really, no.

MACMILLAN   Why not?

LADY DOROTHY   I knew he found me attractive.

MACMILLAN   How did you know?

LADY DOROTHY   I just did.

MACMILLAN   How?

LADY DOROTHY   I sensed it.

MACMILLAN   And him — did you find him attractive?

LADY DOROTHY   Yes.

MACMILLAN   Did you know he wanted to seduce you?

LADY DOROTHY   I don't know. Yes. Yes, I suppose so.

MACMILLAN   You had lunch with him, knowing that he wanted to seduce you, and knowing that you found him attractive?

LADY DOROTHY   Yes.

MACMILLAN   And knowing that I was away?

LADY DOROTHY   Yes.

MACMILLAN   Didn't it occur to you to say no?

LADY DOROTHY   No.

MACMILLAN   Didn't you see where it might lead?

LADY DOROTHY   Well of course.

MACMILLAN   So why did you go?

LADY DOROTHY   Oh, Harold! — only you could ask such a stupid question.

[*Pause.*]

MACMILLAN   Are you in love with him?

LADY DOROTHY   Yes.

MACMILLAN   And he with you?

LADY DOROTHY   Yes.

MACMILLAN   Has he told you so?

LADY DOROTHY   Of course.

[*Pause.*]

MACMILLAN   I thought we were happy together.

[LADY DOROTHY *looks at him, but says nothing.*]

I love you.

[*No response.*]

You know that.

LADY DOROTHY   Yes.

MACMILLAN   I love you with all my heart.

LADY DOROTHY   Yes, yes, I know.

MACMILLAN So why — why have you — why did you look for somebody else?

LADY DOROTHY I didn't look for him. It wasn't like that.

[*Pause.*]

MACMILLAN What made you fall in love with him?

LADY DOROTHY Please stop asking me all these questions.

MACMILLAN He's very good-looking. Was it that?

LADY DOROTHY Please, Harold.

MACMILLAN I need to know.

LADY DOROTHY He makes me laugh.

[MACMILLAN *stares at her.*]

MACMILLAN What?

LADY DOROTHY He makes me laugh. That's why I fell in love with him.

MACMILLAN What do you mean?

LADY DOROTHY Just that.

MACMILLAN He makes you laugh?

LADY DOROTHY Yes.

MACMILLAN You mean he tells jokes?

[*No response.*]

But we laugh. We laugh a lot.

LADY DOROTHY Not in the same way.

MACMILLAN What do you mean?

LADY DOROTHY Do stop saying that.

[*Pause.*]

MACMILLAN It's my fault. I know that. I'm not blaming you. I've been neglectful. It's been a bad year. The damn election. I've been so preoccupied.

LADY DOROTHY It's nothing to do with that.

MACMILLAN What, then?

[LADY DOROTHY *hesitates.*]

What?

LADY DOROTHY You love me as a companion. As the mother of your children. He loves me completely.

MACMILLAN So do I.

LADY DOROTHY Not in the same way.

MACMILLAN He loves you as a mistress.

LADY DOROTHY Yes.

[*The problem is physical love; they both know this, but neither can speak directly and frankly about it.*]

MACMILLAN Is that so very important to you?

[*There is no need for her to reply; he knows the answer.*]

It won't last.

LADY DOROTHY How do you know?

MACMILLAN It never does.

LADY DOROTHY Harold: you don't understand these things. You never will.

[*Pause.*]

MACMILLAN So you had lunch with him in February.

LADY DOROTHY Yes.

MACMILLAN Did you become lovers straightaway?

LADY DOROTHY No, no, of course not.

MACMILLAN But it was in your mind...?

LADY DOROTHY Harold. Please.

MACMILLAN   You met him, you went on meeting him, you
would come home to me and to the children with
these thoughts in your head.

[*No response.*]

No doubt we would have dinner and talk about
the election campaign. Or perhaps we motored
down to Birch Grove. Perhaps I stood at the window and watched you in the garden. And all the
time, these thoughts were in your head.

[*No response.*]

How could you do such a thing, Dorothy? We
have so much that is precious to both of us.

LADY DOROTHY   Don't lecture me, Harold. I'm not in the mood to
be lectured.

[*Pause. They stand very still, facing each other.*]

You think I'm being cruel. I'm being honest.
You're always telling me how much you value
my honesty. Very well. This is the truth. I love
Bob. I didn't realise it was possible to feel like this.
I think of him constantly. This time tomorrow, I
say to myself, this time tomorrow, I'll be with him
again. Or this time the day after tomorrow. Or
this time the day after the day after tomorrow.
It's like a schoolgirl crush, only much stronger
and much more — much more grown-up. It
doesn't mean I've stopped loving you. I have no
passion for you. But I love you. You can love
more than one person at the same time, but passion cannot be shared. [*Pause.*] You ask me if he
loves me and I say, yes, yes, he loves me, and I
think he does, but I can never be sure. He's faithful to me now, or so he says, but I don't think he'll

be faithful for long, he's far too independent. But I don't care about that. I don't care about the future. Bob says love affairs are different from ordinary life because one lives always in the present — no past, no future, always in the present. [*Pause.*] For a few months, for a year or so, I think we were happy, you and I. You loved me very much and I loved you loving me. I didn't understand then how powerful she is — your mother — how dominant. Don't interrupt. Let me talk. The first time I realised the truth was at our wedding. I glanced across the aisle. I thought she was looking at me. I smiled at her. She ignored me — or so I thought. But it wasn't that. She didn't even see me. Her eyes were fixed on you. It was frightening. I've never seen such a look of triumph — of total possession. Don't interrupt, Harold. I've tried to like her. But I can't. She's a snob, she's selfish, and she's ruthless. I hate her. [*Pause.*] I never thought, it never occurred to me, what would happen when we had children of our own. It dawned on me only gradually. I knew — at least, I felt — something had changed between us, but I couldn't be sure what it was, or why, or whether it was just a passing phase. Then, one weekend, all was made clear. We were at Birch Grove. There was some sort of family party. It may've been a birthday, I forget. Perhaps we were celebrating the rebuilding works. Your mother was talking to you and your brothers. I was playing with the children. Your father had retired to his study, poor man, I remember him telling me how much he dislikes social gatherings, even family ones, such a sweet shy man, I feel sorry for him. So I looked at your mother with her three sons. And there was I with our three children. Two women with their children. Two mothers. Suddenly it all became dreadfully clear. Domestic life was repeating itself, and I was trapped in the process like a fly in a jam pot. Because I had become a mother with three children, I had become — in your eyes, in your perception — I had become like her. No longer a wife, I had become a mother. Her. I think I can see why you find the idea so comforting. It creates the illusion of design, of order where there is none. It makes everything so wonderfully tidy — like the books in your study. [*Pause.*] I went upstairs to our room and was sick until I thought I was going to faint. I came downstairs. Tea was being served. Your brother Arthur took me by the arm. "What is it, Dorothy?" he said, "You don't look very well." "Nonsense," she said — your mother said, "she's always that colour, she's always pale." [*Pause.*] We should never have moved into Birch Grove. Never. It's her house. It always has been. It always will be. She's even planting begonias on the east terrace. Begonias! Like the Pooters in that silly book. Why did she plant begonias? [*Pause.*] Sometimes I think you married me just to please her.

MACMILLAN   You know that's not true.

LADY DOROTHY   Do I?

MACMILLAN   You know it, Dorothy.

LADY DOROTHY   I know nothing. How can we ever be sure about love?

[*They stand motionless, facing each other. Time passes.*]

MACMILLAN   What happens now? What are we going to do?

LADY DOROTHY   I don't know.

MACMILLAN   Do you want a divorce?

LADY DOROTHY   Do you?

MACMILLAN   No. No. Absolutely not.

[*He goes to her and takes her by the hand.*]

Don't leave me. Please, I beg you. I need you so much.

[*She looks at him.*]

LADY DOROTHY   I can't stop seeing Bob.

[*Pause.*]

MACMILLAN   All right.

LADY DOROTHY   I mean that. I have to see him.

MACMILLAN   Yes, all right.

[*Pause.*]

The child. Nobody need know. Unless, of course — unless you feel otherwise.

LADY DOROTHY   We can't make these decisions now.

MACMILLAN   No.

[*Pause. They are both aware that some sort of agreement has been reached.* LADY DOROTHY *withdraws her hand from his grasp. She walks purposefully across the room.*]

Don't go. Please.

LADY DOROTHY   I promised to telephone.

[*She goes to the telephone and lifts the receiver.*

(Chester Square, where the Macmillans lived in 1929, was served by one of the London exchanges where calls were answered automatically by an operator.)]

Yes, could you put me through to Kensington 5032, please?

[She looks at MACMILLAN.*]*

I'm not blaming you. It's nobody's fault. Not mine. Not Bob's. Not yours. Not even your mother's. It just happened.

[The call is answered.]

Bob, it's me — Darling, listen: I've told him — Yes, I had to, there was no avoiding it — Well, upset. Very upset — Bob, darling, I must see you. It's important. I'll come round straightaway — I can't tell you on the telephone. I have to see you. I'll be with you in ten minutes.

[She hangs up. MACMILLAN *is sitting hunched and motionless in a chair.]*

It's his child. I have to see him. I have to tell him.

[She exits.]

*[*MACMILLAN *remains in the chair. He bows his head and weeps. The sunlight fades. The flashback ends.]*

[It is evening again, darker than before. The door opens. Light floods in from the corridor outside.]

*[*RITCHIE *comes in.* MACMILLAN *speaks from the shadows.]*

MACMILLAN   Who is that?

RITCHIE   Sorry, sir, it's me, sir, Ritchie. I didn't mean to disturb you.

MACMILLAN   No, no — it's quite all right, come in.

RITCHIE   I hope you weren't asleep.

MACMILLAN   No, no, just reflecting on the day's events.

RITCHIE   I left my briefcase.

> [RITCHIE *finds his briefcase where he left it. He picks it up.*]

MACMILLAN   I hope you had a good supper.

RITCHIE   I certainly did.

MACMILLAN   Mrs Brennan is a first-class housekeeper. Paddy's damn lucky to have her. Second only to Edith. Edith Baker looks after us at Birch Grove. She's the Lady Bowls Champion of Hampshire. An exceptional woman in every way. Have you seen my wife?

RITCHIE   She's with Mr Widdowes. They're talking to Sir Patrick and some of the guests.

MACMILLAN   Ah, yes.

> [RITCHIE *goes to the door.*]

RITCHIE   Will you be wanting to see me tomorrow, sir?

MACMILLAN   Tomorrow? I shouldn't think so.

RITCHIE   I'm planning to catch the 10:15 train, if that's all right.

MACMILLAN   Yes, yes, that's fine. Switch on the light, would you?

> [RITCHIE *does so.*]

You must make it clear to Sir Roger that I am extremely displeased by his handling of this whole wretched business. Sometimes I think the Security

Service operates in a world entirely removed from reality. What happens if the situation gets out of hand and you can't silence Stephen Ward? Eh? What happens then?

RITCHIE   The police seem pretty confident they'll be able to establish a case against Ward.

MACMILLAN   As a pimp, you mean — living off immoral earnings?

RITCHIE   Yes, sir. Keeping a disorderly house, that sort of thing.

MACMILLAN   It won't be easy to find witnesses. People run for cover when they see a scandal on the horizon.

RITCHIE   There are various ways of gathering information. The police'll keep him under surveillance, tap his phone; I'm sure they'll find sufficient evidence.

MACMILLAN   And if they don't — what then?

RITCHIE   Well. Well, I'm not too sure, sir.

MACMILLAN   Let me tell you. There'll be the most vociferous public outcry. And rightly so. I shall be blamed, of course. I don't mind being blamed. One gets used to it. In this job, one expects to be blamed for almost everything. But I do resent being blamed for the ineptitude and botchery of the Security Service.

> [RITCHIE *stands clutching his briefcase while* MACMILLAN *continues his tirade.*]

You people have no understanding of political realities. When Sir Roger told me he'd caught that awful little man Vassall, he couldn't understand why I wasn't delighted. "But he's a Russian spy," he said, "and we've caught him." So I said to him, "When my gamekeeper shoots a fox, he doesn't go and hang it outside the Master of Foxhounds' drawing room; he buries it out of sight." Catch a spy and you have to have a great public trial. That serves no purpose at all. Nobody praises the Security Service for being efficient — everyone says how hopeless they are. If you discover a spy it's far better to control him, destroy his usefulness, but never bring him to trial. Philby's a good example. If he'd been brought back to England, there'd've been the most almighty rumpus. Endless accusations flying about. A terrible row in the press. The Government could easily have fallen. Far better that he ran away to Moscow. [*Pause.*] The point is, Mr Ritchie: I do not want another debacle with Stephen Ward and Captain Ivanov. Sir Roger and his merry men created this situation; it's up to them to solve it.

RITCHIE   Yes, sir.

[MACMILLAN *softens his tone a little.*]

MACMILLAN   I'm not blaming you personally for any of this. I just want to make sure you understand. When you get back to London, they're bound to ask you for my reactions. I don't want there to be any misunderstandings. Is that clear?

RITCHIE   Yes, sir.

MACMILLAN   Good.

[*He lightens the atmosphere with a smile.*]

So you're not flying back?

RITCHIE   Never again, sir, not in one of those little planes.

MACMILLAN   You're very wise. I was once in a plane that crashed. It was during the war. 1943. Algiers. It

didn't take off properly. Taxied down the run-
way, crashed, and burst into flames.

RITCHIE   Were you hurt?

MACMILLAN   Yes, quite badly burned. It was very curious.
They took me to hospital, and when I woke up a
nurse asked me if I wanted to send a message to
anyone. I said, "Yes, to my mother." But she'd
been dead seven years. I thought I was back in
the Somme, in the clearing hospital where I'd
been taken in 1916. Strange, isn't it?

[LADY DOROTHY *comes in with* WIDDOWES. *She
is wearing a man's cardigan over her evening
dress.*]

LADY DOROTHY   I've just spent thirty-five minutes talking to one
of the most boring women I've ever met.

MACMILLAN   Couldn't you run away?

LADY DOROTHY   I tried to. She pursued me. A tall woman in a
purple dress. Did you see her?

MACMILLAN   Don't think so.

LADY DOROTHY   It turns out she's an Old Penrhosian.

MACMILLAN   A what?

LADY DOROTHY   She went to a school called Penrhos College in
Colwyn Bay. Don't you remember? They were
evacuated to Chatsworth during the war. [*to*
RITCHIE] Chatsworth was my home, you see, I
lived there for over twenty years. [*to* MACMILLAN]
She was quite well-meaning, I suppose — but a
tremendous snob. She kept raising her voice so
everyone could hear her talking about "Your
mother, the dear Duchess." Staying at Chatsworth seems to have been the high spot of her
life, poor thing. She said she slept in the Music

Room, which was turned into a dormitory for fifteen girls, and she made a great point of telling me how cold it was in the winter and how she'd had to wear a balaclava helmet in bed. So I said to her, "I was born in that house," I said, "I don't need to be told how cold it is." Was that hideously impolite?

WIDDOWES   Not in the least.

LADY DOROTHY   I think it was.

WIDDOWES   You were charming to her.

LADY DOROTHY   I thought she'd never stop talking.

MACMILLAN   How did you manage to escape?

LADY DOROTHY   Entirely thanks to Oliver. They're getting the barn ready for dancing, so he swept me away in the general commotion of shifting tables and so on.

MACMILLAN   How's old McFee?

LADY DOROTHY   Enjoying himself enormously.

MACMILLAN   I say 'old' McFee — he's not much older than I am.

LADY DOROTHY   Now don't start pretending you're an old man. [to RITCHIE] He does it all the time. [to MACMILLAN] You're as fit as a fiddle. The doctor says you've got the blood pressure of a man of thirty. [to RITCHIE] My husband's a born actor. He can't wait to start playing the part of an old codger. [to WIDDOWES] You must make sure he doesn't. Be firm with him. [to MACMILLAN] It's nonsense for you to talk about getting old. Look how hard you work.

MACMILLAN   A man cannot become young by over-exerting himself. Who said that?

LADY DOROTHY   No idea.

RITCHIE   Hazlitt.

WIDDOWES   Chesterton.

MACMILLAN   Benjamin Jowett. Jowett of Balliol. Much admired for his aphorisms and Greek scholarship. He once said: "Never explain; never apologise; never repeat the mistake." Not a bad motto for a life in politics.

> [LADY DOROTHY *turns to* RITCHIE *with a bright social smile.*]

LADY DOROTHY   I gather you're a spy, Mr Ritchie.

RITCHIE   Well, no, not exactly.

MACMILLAN   He works for MI5. Not the same thing at all.

LADY DOROTHY   Oh, I thought it was.

RITCHIE   MI5 deals with counter-intelligence in the UK, MI6 operates overseas.

LADY DOROTHY   And what is your particular field, or shouldn't I ask?

RITCHIE   D1(c), counter-espionage, Soviet division.

LADY DOROTHY   How very fascinating. How does one get a job like that?

RITCHIE   My father was a policeman, with Special Branch. He had friends in MI5, and when I left university he arranged an introduction.

LADY DOROTHY   Are you armed? Do you have a gun?

RITCHIE   Oh no.

LADY DOROTHY   Unlike the French. When de Gaulle came to Birch Grove his secret service people were armed to the teeth.

MACMILLAN   It was like a private army.

LADY DOROTHY [*to* RITCHIE] One kept bumping into them all over the place. Hiding behind bushes, skulking in the tennis courts, standing on the garage roof.

MACMILLAN He arrived at Gatwick with his own doctors, his own nurse, even his own surgeon.

LADY DOROTHY [*to* RITCHIE] Somebody rang up and said, "What are we going to do about the General's blood?" I had no idea what he was talking about. Apparently de Gaulle is so frightened of being assassinated that he always travels with bottles of blood for transfusion purposes. These bottles have to be kept at a certain temperature, in the fridge, you see, so I went along to the kitchen and had a look in the fridge and found it was full of haddock and things for the weekend, so I said, "Well I'm sorry, it's full." We had to get another fridge — do you remember? — we put it in the coach house.

MACMILLAN It was a very trying weekend. [*to* WIDDOWES] You were there, weren't you?

WIDDOWES I was.

LADY DOROTHY Where did you sleep?

WIDDOWES In a box-room filled with old copies of *Country Life.*

LADY DOROTHY Oh dear. [*to* RITCHIE] Would you mind ringing for Mrs Brennan? There's a bell by the fireplace.

[RITCHIE *rings the bell.*]

MACMILLAN [*to* RITCHIE] De Gaulle is like Winston. He won't give way an inch during a discussion, but a few minutes later he'll suddenly produce one of your ideas and pretend he's just thought of it himself.

LADY DOROTHY He's got very big feet.

MACMILLAN   Enormous.

LADY DOROTHY   And he always wears his trousers hitched up so they look even bigger.

MACMILLAN   [*to* RITCHIE] Mr Blake, our head keeper, was very distressed. Police dogs were patrolling through the woods, getting into the coverts, disturbing the pheasants. "This has got to stop," said Blake. I tried to tell him that a great international occasion was taking place and that the President of France was our guest, but Blake was not at all impressed. "Either he goes or I go," he said — "and I've been here thirty-five years." One of the police alsatians bit a *Daily Mail* man in the behind. I was delighted.

[MRS BRENNAN *enters.*]

LADY DOROTHY   Mrs Brennan, dear, I'm going to have an early night. Would you be kind enough to bring me a cup of tea and some digestive biscuits?

MRS BRENNAN   Yes, milady.

LADY DOROTHY   What about you, Harold?

MACMILLAN   Oliver and I are going to have a glass of brandy. You too, Ritchie, if you'd like one.

RITCHIE   No, thank you, sir — I think I'll go to bed as well.

LADY DOROTHY   Yes, I think you should. It's not a good idea to drink late at night if one's had an upset tummy. How are you feeling now?

RITCHIE   Much better, thank you. [*to* MRS BRENNAN] The supper was delicious.

MRS BRENNAN   Thank you, sir.

[LADY DOROTHY *extends her hand to be shaken.*
RITCHIE *takes the hint: it is time for him to go.*]

LADY DOROTHY	I'm so pleased to have met you, Mr Ritchie. Don't forget to look at the gardens before you leave.
RITCHIE	I certainly will. [*to* MACMILLAN] I'll say goodnight, sir.
MACMILLAN	Goodnight.
RITCHIE	[*to* WIDDOWES] Goodnight.
WIDDOWES	We'd better talk when we're both back in London. Will you ring me at the office?
RITCHIE	I will. Goodnight.
WIDDOWES	Goodnight.
	[RITCHIE *exits.*]
MRS BRENNAN	Can I get anything for you, sir?
MACMILLAN	No, thank you.
MRS BRENNAN	[*to* LADY DOROTHY] Shall I bring your tea up straightaway?
LADY DOROTHY	Yes, please, if you would.
	[MRS BRENNAN *goes to the door.*]
MRS BRENNAN	[*to* WIDDOWES] Goodnight, sir.
WIDDOWES	Goodnight.
MRS BRENNAN	[*to* MACMILLAN] Goodnight, sir.
MACMILLAN	Goodnight, Mrs Brennan.
	[MRS BRENNAN *exits. The door closes.*]
LADY DOROTHY	[*to* WIDDOWES] May I see Mr Profumo's letter?
WIDDOWES	Of course.
	[*He takes the letter from his briefcase.* LADY DOROTHY *puts on her spectacles and takes the letter from* WIDDOWES.]
LADY DOROTHY	Thank you.

[She takes the letter from the envelope and reads it aloud.]

Dear Prime Minister,

You will recollect that on March the twenty-second following certain allegations made in Parliament, I made a personal statement.

At that time rumour had charged me with assisting in the disappearance of a witness and with being involved in some possible breach of security.

So serious were these charges that I allowed myself to think that my personal association with that witness, which had also been the subject of rumour, was, by comparison, of minor importance only.

In my statement I said there had been no impropriety in this association. To my very deep regret I have to admit that this was not true, and that I misled you, and my colleagues, and the House.

I ask you to understand that I did this to protect, as I thought, my wife and family, who are equally misled, as were my professional advisers.

I have come to realise that, by this deception, I have been guilty of a grave misdemeanour, and despite the fact there is no truth whatever in the other charges, I cannot remain a member of your Administration, nor of the House of Commons. I cannot tell you of my deep remorse for the embarrassment I have caused to you, to my colleagues in the Government, to my constituents and to the party which I have served for the past twenty-five years.

> [*Pause.*]

Poor Jack. Poor man.

> [*She folds the letter and returns it to* WIDDOWES.]

I'm sure it's all a Russian plot.

MACMILLAN Yes, I was telling him.

LADY DOROTHY They want to get rid of Harold, you see.

MACMILLAN Oliver is sceptical.

LADY DOROTHY Are you?

WIDDOWES A little.

LADY DOROTHY It makes perfect sense to me. The Russians are frightened of Harold's friendship with President Kennedy. America and England, you see, getting closer together. They want to put a stop to it, so they concoct a plan to bring down the Government and get rid of Harold. Doesn't that make sense to you?

WIDDOWES Well, yes, I suppose it's possible.

LADY DOROTHY More than possible.

> [MACMILLAN *wants to bring this conversation to an end.*]

MACMILLAN [*to* LADY DOROTHY] We'll talk to the Security people about it.

LADY DOROTHY Will you? I wish you would.

MACMILLAN I will.

LADY DOROTHY [*to* WIDDOWES] It's so very upsetting for Harold. He's extremely fond of Jack Profumo.

WIDDOWES We all are. He's a charming man.

MACMILLAN Charming, intelligent, the most promising politician of his generation.

LADY DOROTHY   It's just so awful. Why do these things have to happen? His lovely wife. How ghastly for her. [*to* MACMILLAN] I gather there was a message from Sarah?

MACMILLAN   Yes, she's staying in Geneva for a few more days. [*to* WIDDOWES] Isn't that right?

WIDDOWES   So she said.

LADY DOROTHY   [*to* MACMILLAN] I think you should telephone the doctor. We don't know what's going on. I don't trust these clinics. Full of quacks. And they cost a fortune.

MACMILLAN   The money doesn't matter. If it helps the poor child, I don't mind paying.

LADY DOROTHY   She's got to pull herself together. She's thirty-three — not a poor child any more. Just weak and self-indulgent. [*to* WIDDOWES] It's the sort of thing the newspapers would love to get hold of. I worry so much. It'd damage Harold quite dreadfully.

[*She goes to the door.*]

When are you going back to London?

WIDDOWES   I suppose about lunch time.

LADY DOROTHY   Oh good, I'll see you in the morning. [*to* MACMILLAN] Don't stay up too late. If you can't sleep, take a Veganin. [*to* WIDDOWES] Goodnight, Oliver.

WIDDOWES   Goodnight, Lady Dorothy.

LADY DOROTHY   Goodnight, Harold.

MACMILLAN   Goodnight.

[LADY DOROTHY *exits.*]

[MACMILLAN *walks to the drinks table.*]

I don't like Veganin. It makes me depressed. Brandy or Scotch?

WIDDOWES   I've been drinking gin.

MACMILLAN   That was before your supper. A brandy won't do you any harm. [*He pours two brandies.*] I can just imagine what the press'll make of all this. The usual barrage of sanctimonious, hypocritical claptrap. "There's nothing so ridiculous as the British public in one of its periodical fits of morality." Macaulay was right. Soda?

WIDDOWES   Please.

[MACMILLAN *squirts soda into the brandies and gives one to* WIDDOWES.]

MACMILLAN   Odd, isn't it, how fate brought them together. The tart. The Russian. The pimp. Jack Profumo. It's hard to imagine a more disparate dramatis personae. And yet, because of an unforeseeable series of random events, they have all become leading players in the same drama — sharing the same spotlight, as it were — and as a result their lives have been changed forever. Changed irreversibly. What a capricious thing it is. Life, fate, chance, whatever. You think your foothold is secure, and then, whoops, over you go, tripped up yet again. [*Pause.*] What makes God laugh?

[WIDDOWES *is puzzled.*]

WIDDOWES   What makes God laugh?

MACMILLAN   It's a joke, a riddle.

WIDDOWES   What makes God laugh...? I've no idea.

MACMILLAN   People making plans.

[WIDDOWES *laughs.*]

Haven't you heard that before?

WIDDOWES   No.

MACMILLAN   Hideously true, I'm sure. I've always lived my life on the assumption that things never turn out as you expect. Take it as it comes. That's the only way. I never thought I'd be Prime Minister, never. Rab did, he fully expected it, poor old Rab. Big mistake. Expect nothing and you won't be disappointed. [*A chuckle.*] It's like that limerick Clem Attlee wrote about himself:

Few thought he was even a starter;
There were many who thought themselves
        smarter;
But he ended PM,
CH and OM,
An Earl and a Knight of the Garter.

[WIDDOWES *laughs.* MACMILLAN *sits and sips his brandy.*]

How long've you known Paddy?

WIDDOWES   We were at school together.

MACMILLAN   I knew his father. I often came up to shoot some grouse. My idea of a perfect holiday. What are your plans this summer?

WIDDOWES   Italy. We're staying with some friends near Orvieto.

MACMILLAN   Italy. Yes. I don't see the point of it. If you go to Venice or Florence you might just as well be at Victoria Station. Masses of tourists everywhere. Germans in shorts. Ghastly. No, no, this is the place for me. There's a marvellous sense of continuity. I find that very reassuring. [*Pause.*] I'm increasingly aware that the world has changed. Is changing. Do you think it is? Or is it yet another sign of growing old?

[WIDDOWES *does not reply. He knows* MAC-
MILLAN *is happy to ramble on, exploring his
thoughts and ideas.*]

A doctor was telling me that the decline into old
age is not a steady sloping path but a number of
sudden — and sometimes jolting — downward
steps with a plateau in between. I'm sure it's the
same with the body politic. Societies change suddenly, often drastically, and then continue with
a period of relative stability. Life changes all the
time, of course, but it seems to me there are certain moments when the changes are substantial
and significant. I feel we're living at such a time
now. I feel it very strongly. And I don't mean all
that balderdash about Great Britain losing an
empire and not finding a role, or whatever it was
Dean Acheson said. Conceited ass. It's something
more profound than that. Something deeper. The
last time I was aware of this happening was in
1914. The world, our world, was a different place
before the war.

WIDDOWES   What about Hitler and 1939? Wasn't that also a
time of great change?

MACMILLAN   That was different. Things did change, of course,
but that was because of outside events. Our lives
were changed because of external dangers. What
I'm talking about is a change from within. When
I look back to my childhood and adolescence,
one's experience of life was entirely different.
Entirely different. Talleyrand said that no one
who had not lived in France before the Revolu-
tion could have understood or have enjoyed *la
douceur de vivre.* The same applies to anyone who
cannot remember England before the First World

War. Nothing to do with wealth or luxury or anything like that. There was a sense of peace — now lost, I'm afraid — of peace and security. Of spiritual repose.

WIDDOWES   Halcyon days.

MACMILLAN   That makes it sound sentimentally perfect, which it certainly wasn't. When I was at day-school in Cadogan Place, I was often haunted by a strange fear — the feeling that something unpleasant was about to happen — the awareness of some kind of mysterious power which I felt sure would get me in the end. A psychiatrist once told me it's a form of depression. Winston suffers in a similar fashion — though far more acutely. He calls it the 'black dog'. I've learnt to live with it. Reading Jane Austen is a great help at such times. Jane Austen or Trollope. [*He sips his brandy.*] I remember crying on my first day at prep school. An older boy tried to comfort me. "Don't cry," he said, "your situation is bad, but not desperate." [*He laughs.*] Bad — but not desperate! One might say the same now. [*Pause.*] The 'black dog' followed me to Eton. It was not a happy time. I had no sense of purpose. The 'black dog' was with me a very great deal. Did you enjoy school?

WIDDOWES   Yes, I did rather.

MACMILLAN   I left when I was seventeen. I caught pneumonia. It affected my heart. So my mother decided I should study at home for a Balliol scholarship. She was an American, my mother. Fiercely nonconformist. A formidable woman. She and my father met in Paris, where she was studying music and art. They were the most ill-assorted couple

I've ever known. How and why they fell in love is a complete mystery. But they did, and they remained married — I think happily — for over fifty years. Anyway, after much consideration, my mother chose Ronnie Knox to be my tutor. Ronnie was only twenty-two and already greatly admired by his contemporaries. We became the best of friends. It was the first real friendship I'd ever known. We were devoted to each other. He was a very sweet man. A saint, really. A saint with a sense of humour. We were always laughing. He loved bananas. He ate bananas every day. He regarded bananas as the ideal fruit since they required neither plate nor knife and fork and could be eaten in any posture. Dear Ronnie. The only man I've ever met who was completely tone deaf. He couldn't even recognise *God Save the King.* He was a very devout Anglo-Catholic. Later, of course, he converted to Rome and became a priest. I was very drawn to the Roman Catholic church. One day, Ronnie took me to an Anglo-Catholic mass. When my mother discovered this, she dismissed him immediately. Immediately. She didn't even give us the chance to say goodbye. I was devastated. So, I think, was he. But then, the following year, I went up to Oxford and we were able to renew our friendship. Ronnie was then Chaplain at Trinity. I was at Balliol. It was the happiest time of my life. Sligger Urquhart was Junior Bursar. A wonderful man. Sligger Urquhart. The first Catholic don at Oxford since the Reformation. Not an outstanding scholar, but a man of the greatest kindness and generosity of spirit. He had a chalet near Mont Blanc, and a group of us went there for a summer holiday, a reading party. We talked, we climbed, we read, we argued. I remember waking one morning and looking out at the mountains and the clear, cloudless sky and thinking: I am now, at this moment, perfectly happy. Within a few months, war was declared and that golden age had gone forever. [*He sips his brandy.*] I didn't see much of Ronnie after that. We went our different ways. Six years ago somebody told me he was very ill. Cancer of the liver. I got in touch with him and arranged for him to see my doctor for a second opinion. He came up from Mells, where he was living, and stayed with us at Downing Street. The news wasn't good. The diagnosis was confirmed. I went with him to Paddington to see him off on the train. I shook his hand and wished him a comfortable journey. "It'll be a very long one," he said. I watched him as he walked away along the platform. I thought of him as he once was. Of our days in Oxford, where the sun rose over Wadham and set over Worcester. [*He sighs. Pause. He sips his brandy.*] A few years ago, Winston said to Rab, "I feel like an aeroplane at the end of its flight, in the dusk, with petrol running out, in search of a safe landing." [*Pause.*] His doctor tells me the old boy is in poor shape. Unmoving, unspeaking, incontinent, consumed by melancholy. The 'black dog' has got him in the end. [*Pause. He chuckles.*] Winston's doctor is Lord Moran. He once boasted that he was often present when history was made. "Not actually present," somebody said, "but he was invited to luncheon afterwards."

[WIDDOWES *laughs.*]

Why was I talking about Ronnie Knox?

WIDDOWES You were saying how the world changed in 1914.

MACMILLAN Ah yes, Well it did. And it's the same now. I feel it very strongly. And not necessarily a change for the better. By no means a change for the better. The wild waters are upon us. [*He rises to his feet and picks up his brandy glass.*] Do you want another drink?

WIDDOWES No, thank you, sir.

MACMILLAN One needs a spiritual centre. A sense of something more substantial than making money and self-advancement. It's that, I think, we're in danger of losing. Maybe it's already lost. What do you think? I wonder if it is.

WIDDOWES Possibly. I hope not.

MACMILLAN So do I.

[*He walks to the drinks table and pours himself another brandy and soda.*]

My father was a Christian Socialist. So was Ronnie Knox. They both loathed the materialist Liberalism that seemed to dominate this country. I was brought up in their tradition. The English radical tradition. One was appalled by the suffering and misery of the poor. One was angered by the apparent incapacity of our economic society to do anything about it. That's why I went into politics. It seemed the only possible thing to do. And I'm sure many young people feel the same today. But underpinning my actions, and my resolve, was a deep and abiding religious faith. And it was this faith that gave me strength. It provided the foundation upon which I could build my life — a foundation that I fear very few can rely on today. But perhaps I'm wrong. Am I?

WIDDOWES   Religion is not the only reliable foundation.

MACMILLAN   No, no, I'm not saying it is.

WIDDOWES   Perhaps humanitarian concerns now provide the strength you found in the Church.

MACMILLAN   Perhaps.

WIDDOWES   Isn't that possible?

MACMILLAN   Absolutely. [*He sips his brandy.*] I suppose what I regret is the absence of mystery. Of something beyond human understanding. The absence of God, I suppose.

WIDDOWES   Someone suggested that God might be teaching man to live without God.

MACMILLAN   What an extraordinary idea.

WIDDOWES   Not mine, alas.

MACMILLAN   God teaching man to live without God. Is that a lesson we want to learn?

WIDDOWES   It depends, I suppose, on the sort of person you are. I used to have faith; I was brought up to believe; it was important to me. I don't know why I stopped. There was no great flash of rejection or revelation. It just occurred to me, one day, quite calmly, that I no longer believed. And then, of course, it seemed incredible that I ever had. It isn't easy, living without faith. I miss the grand design. I miss the consolation. When Isobel was first taken ill, I longed for the embrace of the Church. I longed for the solace of prayer. But it had flown away. Gone for ever. I suppose my life seems harsher without God. But, in a strange way, richer. One feels more completely a human being — more isolated, if you like — no longer a child of God.

[MACMILLAN *is astonished.*]

MACMILLAN Do you enjoy that?

WIDDOWES Not enjoy, no — but I find it rather invigorating.

MACMILLAN I don't have that sort of courage. I need religion. I need its strength, I need its comfort. Without God, I would feel very alone. [*He walks to the window and looks out.*] I know non-believers say religion provides nothing more than easy comfort. Well, what's wrong with that? — even if it were true, which I don't think it is, not for a moment. In this life we need all the comfort we can get. [*Pause. He takes a sip of brandy.*] She still sees him. Boothby. If they don't meet, they talk on the telephone. Every day. I hear her voice, I hear her laughter. Every day for thirty years. [*Pause.*] He likes men as well. Or so they say. Is that true, do you think, or is it just a malicious rumour? Working-class boys. [*Pause.*] When Dorothy told me about the affair I felt utterly destroyed. We'd been married less than ten years. Three children. Our life seemed perfect. I had no idea anything might be wrong. [*Pause.*] For a time, I felt I couldn't go on. The doctor called it 'nervous prostration'. Mama sent me to a sanatorium near Munich. The walls were painted cream. I stared at the walls every day, all day. I found it very restful. [*Pause.*] He wrote and asked me for a life peerage. People thought I'd be outraged; in fact, I was mildly amused. If he wants the House of Lords, I thought, why not let him have it? Baron Boothby of Buchan and Rattray Head. Characteristically overblown and flamboyant. [*Pause.*] Dorothy begged me for a divorce. And he was desperate to marry her, no doubt about that. I refused to comply. Rightly, I believe. The children would have suffered. One was aware of their unhappiness, of course, but it would've been worse, I think, had we divorced. For them and for me.

> [*Pause.* WIDDOWES *stands staring at* MACMILLAN, *not knowing what to do or say.*]

I smile at Sarah and I see his eyes smiling back at me. It'd be easier, perhaps, if I hated her. But I love her so much. My belovèd daughter. But not my daughter. You were right to talk of the avoidance of pain. There's nothing more important.

> [*He turns from the window and sees* WIDDOWES' *anguished expression.*]

Forgive me, Oliver. I shouldn't talk of these things. They are private and should remain so. [*He smiles and takes a step towards the door.*] Time for bed. An early night'll do me good. I'm halfway through *Cousin Henry*. Do you know it?

WIDDOWES   *Cousin Henry?*

MACMILLAN   Trollope. Uncommon, as booksellers say.

WIDDOWES   I've never even heard of it.

MACMILLAN   Very good. You'd enjoy it.

> [*He goes to open the door.*]

WIDDOWES   Should we do something about the letter?

MACMILLAN   What letter?

WIDDOWES   Jack Profumo's letter.

MACMILLAN   Oh yes. I'd better dictate a reply. Do you have some paper?

[WIDDOWES *takes a pad from his briefcase and a fountain pen from his inside pocket.*]

WIDDOWES   Paper and a pen.

[MACMILLAN *thinks for a moment, then he dictates the following.*]

MACMILLAN   "Dear Profumo, I have read your letter of the fourth of June with deep regret. Full stop. This is a great tragedy for you, comma, your family and your friends. Full stop. Nevertheless, comma, I am sure you will understand that in the circumstances, comma, I have no alternative but to advise the Queen to accept your resignation. Yours very sincerely."

You can get it typed up in the morning. I'll sign it.

[*The door opens.* LADY DOROTHY *enters. She is wearing a man's plaid dressing-gown.*]

LADY DOROTHY   Did I leave my glasses somewhere?

WIDDOWES   You did.

[*He picks them up and gives them to her.*]

LADY DOROTHY   I've been hunting high and low. Thank you, Oliver. I couldn't think what I'd done with them.

MACMILLAN   We've hunted for her spectacles all over the world.

LADY DOROTHY   We have indeed.

MACMILLAN   Cape Town.

LADY DOROTHY   Washington.

MACMILLAN   Ghana — when you had toothache.

LADY DOROTHY   And that dreadful state dinner — India, some-where — Delhi, it must've been — there was a very grand state dinner and I was sitting next to a man who looked like a cross between Liberace and Little Lord Fauntleroy.

MACMILLAN   President Sukarno.

LADY DOROTHY   President Sukarno. I can never remember his name. We were all fellow guests — was it Delhi?

MACMILLAN   It was.

LADY DOROTHY   Mr Nehru was the host — utterly charming and civilised — but the food he served was deplorable. Even Harold thought so, and he doesn't give a hoot about food.

MACMILLAN   It was like eating in a fifth-rate boarding house.

LADY DOROTHY   So there we were, sitting down to this awful meal, and I realised I'd left my spectacles in the bed-room. It was bad enough eating such terrible food, but not being able to see it made it a hun-dred times worse. So I sent one of the servants to fetch my glasses, back he came, I put them on, and as soon as I saw the food I immediately wished I hadn't.

               [*Laughter.* LADY DOROTHY *goes to the door. Pause.*]

               [*to* MACMILLAN] Did you take a Veganin?

MACMILLAN   No, actually, I — no.

LADY DOROTHY   I think you should. You'll lie in bed and worry about Jack Profumo. A couple of Veganin'll make you sleep.

               [MACMILLAN *smiles at* WIDDOWES.]

MACMILLAN   What would I do without her?

LADY DOROTHY   You'd do very nicely.

MACMILLAN   I doubt it.

> [*He follows her to the door, but pauses for a moment as he hears the sound of a Scottish country dance band playing 'Broon's Reel' in the barn.*]

Listen. They're dancing.

> [MACMILLAN, LADY DOROTHY *and* WIDDOWES *listen to the reel.* MACMILLAN *opens the door.*]

Goodnight, Oliver. Sleep well.

WIDDOWES   Goodnight, sir.

LADY DOROTHY   Goodnight.

WIDDOWES   Goodnight, Lady Dorothy.

> [MACMILLAN *and* LADY DOROTHY *exit.*]

> [WIDDOWES *puts the notepad away in his briefcase. He switches off the light, walks to the door and exits.*]

> [*The high-spirited music of the reel can still be heard as darkness fills the empty room.*]

THE END

BIBLIOGRAPHY

Annan, Noel: Our Age (Weidenfeld & Nicolson, 1990).

Benn, Tony: Diaries, 1963-67 (Hutchinson, 1987).

Blom-Cooper, Louis: Law and Morality (Duckworth, 1976).

Booker, Christopher: The Neophiliacs (Collins, 1969).

Boothby, Lord: Recollections of a Rebel (Hutchinson, 1978).

Brivati, Brian: Hugh Gaitskell (Richard Cohen Books, 1996).

Butler, Lord: The Art of the Possible (Hamish Hamilton, 1971).

Carrington, Lord: Reflect on Things Past (Collins, 1988).

Charlton, Warwick: Stephen Ward Speaks (Today Magazine
        Publications, 1963).

Charmley, John: Duff Cooper (Weidenfeld & Nicolson, 1986).

Charmley, John: A History of Conservative Politics 1900-1996
        (Macmillan, 1996).

Collis, Maurice: Diaries 1949-1969 (Heinemann, 1977).

Cooper, Lady Diana: The Light of Common Day (Hart-Davis, 1959).

Cooper, Duff: Old Men Forget (Hart-Davis, 1953).

Coote, Sir Colin: Editorial (Eyre & Spottiswood, 1965).

Cowles, Fleur: She Made Friends and Kept Them (Harper Collins,
        1996).

Crawford, Iain: The Profumo Affair (White Lodge Books, 1963).

Crossman, Richard: The Backbench Diaries (Book Club Associates,
        1981).

Denning, Lord: Lord Denning's Report (HMSO, 1963).

Devlin, Lord: The Enforcement of Morals (Oxford University Press,
        1965).

Dixon, Patrick: The Truth about Westminster (Kingsway Publications,
        1996).

Edwards, Ruth Dudley: Harold Macmillan, a Life in Pictures
        (Macmillan, 1983).

Egremont, Lord: Wyndham and Children First (Macmillan, 1968).

Elliott, Nicholas: Never Judge a Man by his Umbrella (Michael Russell,
        1991).

Evans, Sir Harold: Downing Street Diary (Hodder & Stoughton, 1981).

Fisher, Nigel: Harold Macmillan (Weidenfeld & Nicolson, 1982).

Fitzgerald, Penelope: The Knox Brothers (Macmillan, 1977).

Gere, J.A. & Sparrow, John: Geoffrey Madan's Notebooks (Oxford University Press, 1981).

Hailsham, Lord: The Door Wherein I Went (Collins, 1975).

Hampshire, Stuart: Public and Private Morality (Cambridge University Press, 1978).

Hampshire, Stuart: Two Theories of Morality (Oxford University Press, 1977).

Henderson, Nicholas: The Private Office (Weidenfeld & Nicolson, 1984).

Hennessy, Peter: Muddling Through (Gollancz, 1996).

Horne, Alistair: Macmillan 1891-1956 (Macmillan, 1988).

Horne, Alistair: Macmillan 1956-1986 (Macmillan, 1989).

Howard, Anthony & West, Richard: The Making of the Prime Minister (Cape, 1965).

Howard, Anthony: RAB: The Life of R.A.Butler (Cape, 1987).

Hutchinson, George: The Last Edwardian at Number 10 (Quartet Books, 1980).

Hughes, Emrys: Macmillan (Allen & Unwin, 1962).

Inglis, Brian: Private Conscience, Public Morality (Deutsch, 1964).

Irving, Clive: Scandal '63 (Heinemann, 1963).

James, Robert Rhodes: Bob Boothby (Hodder & Stoughton, 1991).

Jenkins, Roy: Portraits and Miniatures (Macmillan, 1993).

Keeler, Christine: Nothing But... (New English Library, 1983).

Kennedy, Ludovic: The Trial of Stephen Ward (Gollancz 1964).

Knightley, Phillip & Kennedy, Caroline: An Affair of State (Cape, 1987).

Kilmuir, the Earl of: Political Adventure (Weidenfeld & Nicolson, 1964).

Lamb, Richard: The Macmillan Years (John Murray, 1995).

Leigh, David: The Wilson Plot (Heinemann, 1988).

Levin, Bernard: The Pendulum Years (Cape, 1970).

Macmillan, Harold: Winds of Change (Macmillan, 1966).

Macmillan, Harold: The Blast of War (Macmillan, 1967).

Macmillan, Harold: Tides of Fortune (Macmillan, 1969).

Macmillan, Harold: Riding the Storm (Macmillan, 1971).

Macmillan, Harold: Pointing the Way (Macmillan, 1972).

Macmillan, Harold: At the End of the Day (Macmillan, 1973).

Macmillan, Harold: War Diaries (Macmillan, 1984).

Macmillan, Harold: The Past Masters (Macmillan, 1975).

Macmillan, Harold: The Carlton Lecture, 1982 (Macmillan, 1983).

Macmillan, Harold: Introduction to Geoffrey Madan's Notebooks (Oxford University Press, 1981).

Margalit, Avishai: The Decent Society (Harvard University Press, 1996).

Nicolson, Harold: Diaries and Letters (Collins, 1966-68).

Park, Nancie: School Days at Chatsworth (A Quick & Co, 1986).

Paxman, Jeremy: Friends in High Places (Michael Joseph, 1990).

Phelps, Barry: Power and the Party (Macmillan, 1983).

Pimlott, Ben: Frustrate Their Knavish Tricks (Harper Collins, 1993).

Pincher, Chapman: Their Trade is Treachery (Sidgwick & Jackson, 1981).

Pincher, Chapman: Too Secret too Long (Sidgwick & Jackson, 1984).

Rawls, John: Political Liberalism (Columbia University Press, 1993).

Rice-Davies, Mandy: The Mandy Report (Confidential Publications, 1963).

Rice-Davies, Mandy: Mandy (Michael Joseph, 1980).

Sampson, Anthony: Anatomy of Britain Today (Hodder & Stoughton, 1965).

Sampson, Anthony: Macmillan (Allen Lane, 1967).

Storr, Anthony: Churchill's Black Dog (Collins, 1989).

Summers, Anthony & Dorril, Stephen: Honeytrap (Weidenfeld & Nicolson, 1987).

Thomas, Hugh: The Establishment (Anthony Blond, 1959).

Thorpe, D.R.: Selwyn Lloyd (Cape, 1989).

Thurlow, David: Profumo: The Hate Factor (Robert Hale, 1992).

Turner, John: Macmillan (Longmann, 1994).

Waugh, Evelyn: Ronald Knox (Chapman & Hall, 1959).

West, Nigel: A Matter of Trust (Weidenfeld & Nicolson, 1982).

West, Nigel: Mole-hunt (Weidenfeld & Nicolson, 1987).

West, Rebecca: The New Meaning of Treason (Viking, 1964).

Williams, Bernard: Morality (Cambridge University Press, 1972).

Williams, Bernard: Moral Luck (Cambridge University Press, 1981).

Wright, Peter: Spy Catcher (Viking, 1987).

Young, Wayland: The Profumo Affair (Penguin, 1963).

Ziegler, Philip: Diana Cooper (Hamish Hamilton, 1981).